Photos of Airports: <u>Old</u> Idl...

Hounslow - Heathrow

Croydon
Le Bourget
Schipol
Copenhagen
Stockholm
Karachi
Singapore

La Guardia
Newark
La Guardia
Idlewild (2)

Heathrow   Gilgit
Gatwick   HongKong
Bova Scotland   Melbourne
Orly
Roissy   Calgary
Schiphol   Toronto
Zurich   Prestwick
                  Bermuda
Dubai   Honolulu
Algiers

THE WORLD'S AIRPORTS

UNIFORM WITH THIS BOOK

JOAN BRADBROOKE *The World's Helicopters*

H. F. KING *The World's Bombers*

H. F. KING *The World's Fighters*

H. F. KING *The World's Strike Aircraft*

JOHN STROUD *The World's Airliners*

PUTNAM WORLD AERONAUTICAL LIBRARY

THE WORLD'S
AIRPORTS

JOHN STROUD

THE BODLEY HEAD

LONDON SYDNEY TORONTO

ACKNOWLEDGMENTS

For assistance in the preparation of this book and for kindly supplying photographs thanks are due to: Aéroport de Paris, Air-Alpes, Air Canada, American Airlines, Bermuda News Bureau, British Airports Authority, British European Airways, BOAC, Dallas/Fort Worth Regional Airport Board, *Esso Air World*, Fokker - VFW, The General Electric Co Ltd, Hawker Siddeley Aviation, Michael J. Hooks, International Aeradio Ltd, KLM Royal Dutch Airlines, Marconi's Wireless Telegraph Co Ltd, Jacques Noetinger, Pan American World Airways, Jean Perard, The Port of New York Authority (now renamed The Port Authority of New York and New Jersey), Qantas, Guy Roberty, Sabena, Scandinavian Airlines System, Schiphol Airport Authority, South African Railways, Swissair, *The Times*, Trans World Airlines, and United Air Lines.

© John Stroud 1973
ISBN 0 370 01573 8
Printed Offset Litho and bound in Great Britain for
The Bodley Head Limited
9 Bow Street, London WC2E 7AL
by Cox & Wyman Ltd, Fakenham
Set in Monotype Baskerville
First published 1973

CONTENTS

INTRODUCTION

For the purposes of this book the word airport has been taken to include the great international airports of the world, the smaller airports handling local services, desert and island airstrips, marine airports, heliports, STOLports, altiports, and even airship bases. This very wide interpretation has been made in order to provide the most complete picture of the very varied landing grounds which serve the world's air transport system.

The term airport should, strictly, be limited to an aerodrome at which international services arrive and depart, and where, consequently, customs facilities are provided. However, this limited definition has largely been forgotten and the term is now applied to any aerodrome which handles regular commercial passenger or cargo services.

The number of airports, aerodromes, landing grounds and heliports throughout the world is unknown but adds up to a very large total. They range in size from rough strips a few hundred feet long for fixed-wing aeroplanes, or about 1,600 sq ft (150 sq m) for helicopters, up to giant complexes the size of a city. Some are used for one or two landings a week, or even less, while others such as Chicago's O'Hare Airport handle more than 1,750 take-offs or landings every day with more than thirty million passengers a year using its facilities.

Airports are situated at all elevations from below sea level up to some 14,000 ft (4,250 m) high in the Andes and in climates ranging from the sub-zero temperatures of the Arctic winter to the blazing heat of the tropics.

This book traces the story of the airport from its earliest days when small grass fields sufficed to handle the light-weight low-speed wood and fabric biplanes up to the present when very long concrete runways are required for the operation of 350-ton aeroplanes capable of carrying 500 passengers and crew. There is also a glimpse of the future as new airports are planned and built to handle the volume of world air traffic which is doubling approximately every seven years.

London has been given first place in this work because the first recorded attempt to produce a civil

◄ December twilight at John F. Kennedy International Airport, New York. A Trans World Airlines Boeing 707 stands close to the airline's birdlike terminal which was designed by Eero Saarinen. The control tower is beyond the aircraft.

airport was at Hounslow when scheduled international air services began in 1919, although, technically, the first airports were those used by German Zeppelins before the 1914–18 war, but no scheduled services were operated at that time.

Britain played a prominent part in the development of air transport particularly in establishing long-distance trunk routes for the regular carriage of passengers, and because of the magnitude of this pioneering effort it has been used in this book to illustrate the problems involved in providing airports in widely differing terrain and climates.

Strange as it may now seem, the United States was far behind Europe in the development of regular passenger-carrying air services and for this reason the US airports are not described until Chapter 5. Now United States airlines carry well over half the world's total air traffic and the country's airport system is of great importance. For this reason considerable space has been given to United States airports, and the very large and advanced Dallas/Fort Worth Regional Airport, now under construction,

has been used to give some impression of the airports of the twenty-first century.

In a book of this length it is obviously not possible to describe or even mention many of the world's airports, a selection has had to be made to cover some of the most important as well as those which give a picture of the many types of facilities in use.

It will be seen that throughout this book there is variation in the forms in which measurements have been given. In the case of most European airports, and some others, the metric dimensions have been shown first, with Imperial conversions; elsewhere metric takes second place. There is also some variation in the actual conversions because some rounding off has occurred in what might be termed official figures, such as those used to define the categories for low visibility landing approaches. For much of the world, runway lengths and elevations are quoted in feet and this is the form adopted by International Aeradio's Aerad Flight Guides which are widely used by international airline crews.

1

London's First Airports

The present giant international airports with multiple concrete runways, terminal cities, hangars and engineering bases, hotels, shops, cargo terminals and enormous car parks, have all developed from the primitive grass aerodromes of modest expanse from which the first air services were operated in the years immediately following the 1914–18 war.

The main requirements for an airport have changed little. They are: a level piece of ground providing sufficient room for the landing and take-off runs of the aircraft; reasonably unobstructed approaches so that aircraft can climb away safely after take-off and make their landing approaches safely; space for all the necessary buildings; good access to the cities or communities they serve; and the best possible weather conditions.

Because the early transport aeroplanes required only short landing and take-off runs, the density of traffic was low, and the great expansion of the cities had not taken place, it was possible to site most of the early airports close to the cities they served – some only a tram ride away.

As the aircraft became bigger and heavier and needed longer take-off runs, and as the cities pushed out their boundaries into the country, it frequently became necessary to find new sites on which bigger airports could be built – these factors were to some extent responsible for the fact that over the years more than a dozen airports have been used to serve London. But in some places a wise choice of original siting, or restrictions imposed by terrain have meant that airports have continued to be developed on the original sites – Amsterdam's Schiphol Airport is an example of continual growth on the same site.

Hounslow Aerodrome during the 1914–18 war, shortly before becoming London's
first civil airport. The long hangar, in the row of three,
became the terminal and customs shed.

The history of London's airports serves to illustrate airport development involving a series of sites and in this chapter it is traced from the start of air services in 1919 up to the start of the Second World War in September 1939.

London's first terminal airport was Hounslow Aerodrome on Hounslow Heath close to the southeast corner of the present London Airport at Heathrow. This was a small grass area which had been used as a military aerodrome, and it possessed a number of hangars, mostly of temporary war-time canvas type, and a few barrack units. For commercial use the name HOUNSLOW was laid out in white letters on the grass for identification from the air, and one of the permanent hangars was taken over as a terminal and customs shed. The word 'Customs' was painted in white capitals above one door and its French equivalent, 'Douane', above the other. On one end wall was the title 'Continental Departure Station' – also lettered in French – and on one door was a weather map and a notice board to which were attached meteorological reports and messages.

Civil flying from Hounslow began on 1 May 1919, and scheduled passenger and cargo flights started on 25 August that year when Aircraft Transport and Travel opened a regular London–Paris service using de Havilland 4A and 16 single-engined bi-planes. A French service with Breguet 14s began using Hounslow that September, and the large twin-engined Handley Page O/400s of Handley Page Transport landed at Hounslow to clear customs, although their London terminal was the company's own aerodrome at Cricklewood. S. Instone and Co used Hounslow for their private services from October 1919 and began public services between Hounslow and Paris in February 1920.

Most of the flying was done in daylight and in the beginning without the aid of radio, but a limited system of radio communication came into use at Hounslow in October 1919. A flashing light beacon was switched on if needed and a 70,000 candle-power revolving beacon was installed at the end of 1919.

Although Hounslow was the official customs airport for London, Handley Page Transport operated from Cricklewood. This was a rather confined and none-too-flat area bordering on the old London and North Western Railway line and only about 4 miles (6½ km) up the Edgware Road from Marble Arch. There were a few hangars, again mostly of canvas, and precious little else, but in February 1920 Cricklewood was appointed an Air Port, a customs office was provided and a Civil Aviation Transport Officer installed. Handley Page continued to run its services from Cricklewood until May 1921, after which the aerodrome was used for several years for the testing of new Handley Page aeroplanes.

Hounslow was never really suitable for the operation of air services and at the end of March 1920 it was closed down and operations transferred to Croydon to the south of London. The new site was known as Croydon Aerodrome – The London Terminal Aerodrome, but for several years it was generally referred to as Waddon or Plough Lane. Before airline operations began at Croydon, there had been two adjoining landing grounds on the site – the western one, known as Wallington, had been used by the Royal Flying Corps since 1915, and the eastern area, known as Waddon, served the National Aircraft Factory. The two areas were separated by the north – south Plough Lane.

To the west of Plough Lane were several large war-time hangars and in these were housed the larger transport aircraft. On the same section of Plough Lane, but on its eastern side, a terminal village of wooden huts was erected. This included airline offices, a customs block and, high on stilts, a white-painted wooden control tower. There were also a few canvas hangars for the smaller types of aircraft. To get from the big hangars to the terminal area the aircraft taxi-ed across Plough Lane over a 'level crossing' and past a farm that remained right in the terminal area.

The whole terminal area became a sea of mud in winter and on one occasion one of the canvas hangars collapsed under the weight of snow on its roof, with disastrous consequences for the one and only de Havilland 54 Highclere which was within.

The landing area was undulating and had some soft areas, and these features remained throughout the airport's life. The maximum take-off and landing runs, aligned north–south and northeast–southwest, were about 4,000 ft (1,200 m) and 3,500 ft (1,070 m) respectively although effectively less because of the hill to the south of the airport. The airport was equipped with a 'lighthouse' and floodlight and wireless communication, and air traffic control was developed during the early days on the Plough Lane site. The signal that it was clear to take-off was given to pilots by a man waving a red flag.

The scale of air traffic in those pioneering years is well illustrated by the total of 17,802 flights and 46,966 passengers on cross-Channel routes between August 1919 and March 1924, with Croydon handling 4,665 flights and 14,777 passengers in the year 1923–24 – the only airlines operating there at that time being British, French, Belgian and Dutch. By comparison, Heathrow handled more than 27,000 flights in July 1970 and 62,290 passengers in one day in August that year.

The Air Port of London – Croydon, in the early 1930s. In the centre ▶ is the terminal with administrative offices and control tower, on the left the main hangars, and in the foreground the hotel. The biplane is the Imperial Airways Argosy *City of Coventry* and the monoplane a KLM Fokker F.VIII.

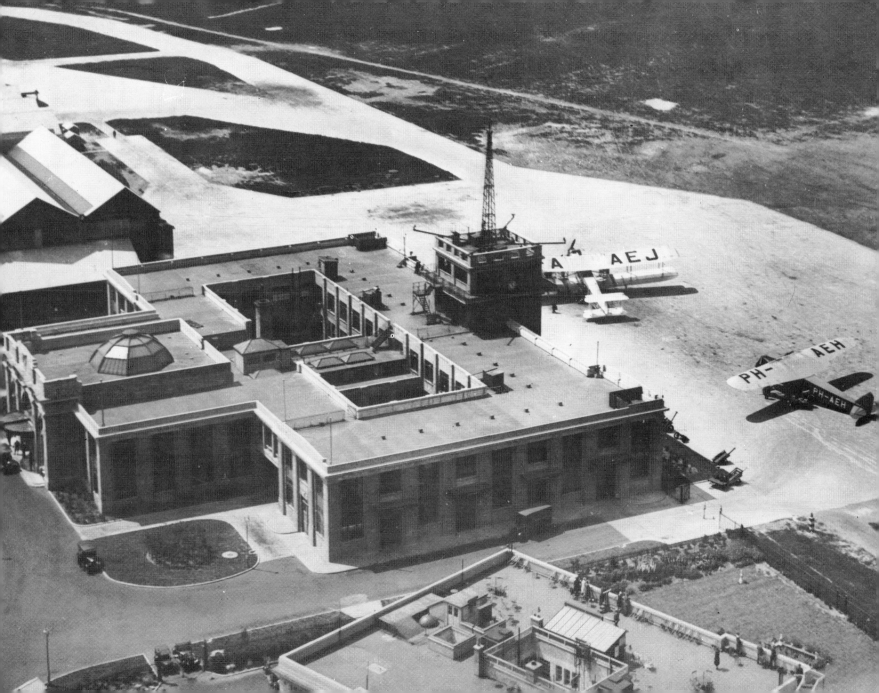

After a few years' operation at the Plough Lane site, it was decided that a much more adequate airport was required and during 1925 work began on a completely new Croydon terminal area and enlargement and improvement of the landing area.

The new terminal area was built on the eastern boundary of the airport alongside the new Purley Way and comprised a terminal building surmounted by a 50-ft (15 m) high control tower, an hotel and, initially, two two-bay hangars each measuring 300 by 150 ft (90 by 45 m). There were also workshops and administrative offices. In front of the terminal and hangars were concrete aprons and these were linked by taxiways.

Under the title Air Port of London, Croydon, the new terminal came into operation at the end of January 1928 although the old Plough Lane control tower remained in use until that April. The official opening was on 2 May. The old terminal was then demolished, Plough Lane closed – although each end still survives as a residential street – and the two landing grounds were joined to form a single area providing a maximum run of about 5,000 ft (1,500 m). More than thirty years later, from the air one could see as markings in the grass the outlines of the old terminal.

Lighting for night operations continued to be developed. Croydon had flashing red boundary lights to mark its extent; non-flashing red lights on all obstructions; a red flashing neon location beacon which under favourable conditions could be seen from 80 miles (130 km) away; landing floodlights, one of which was mobile; and an illuminated wind direction indicator in the form of a letter T. The then conventional 200 ft (60 m) diameter white circle marked the landing area and close to it in capital letters was the name Croydon. Permission to take-off and land was given by signal lamp from the control tower, and a klaxon horn was sounded when an incoming international flight was sighted. At a later date a line of sunken red neon lights, aligned northeast–southwest, was used to assist landings at night and in poor visibility.

Croydon remained the main British airport until the suspension of air services at the outbreak of war in September 1939. By that time quite large four-engined aircraft were using the airport, but few changes had taken place at the airport itself in the past decade. The interior of the terminal had been re-arranged and two large hangars were nearing completion; but otherwise Croydon was the same undulating grass field, long outclassed by some of the airports in continental Europe.

To complete the story of Croydon it should be recorded that the airport was reopened for civil operation on 13 November 1944, when a London–

Liverpool–Belfast service was flown by Railway Air Services. With the ending of the war European and domestic services again worked from Croydon but most of these were transferred to Northolt in 1946, while the long-distance services used Hurn near Bournemouth. The old airport was finally closed on 30 September 1959 – the last service being a flight to Rotterdam by a Morton Air Services de Havilland Heron, appropriately under the command of Capt Geoffrey Last.

It is of interest to recall that, although the distance between Croydon and Paris or Brussels is only a little over 200 miles (320 km), in the early days of air transport many aircraft had to stop for fuel on these short stages. Lympne, near the coast and not far from Folkestone, was used by many aircraft which were short of fuel or encountered bad weather, and before wireless was in regular use cross-Channel aircraft had to circle Lympne to announce their departure or safe arrival, a similar duty being imposed on the other side of the Channel. To cater for bad weather, engine trouble or fuel shortage there were also several emergency landing grounds between Croydon and the coast, these included Penshurst and Marden and they were quite frequently used.

Another London aerodrome which served as an airport was Heston. This was a grass field of modest dimensions, situated just north of the Bath Road and beneath one of the approaches to the present Heathrow. Some domestic services were operated from Heston in the 1930s, mostly to the Isle of Wight and the Channel Islands, and for some time before the 1939–45 war Heston served as the main base of British Airways which operated services to Germany, Scandinavia and Poland. The M4 motorway now ploughs through what was once the landing area.

Two small grass aerodromes in Essex served for a while as airports for London when they were the bases of Hillman's Airways. The first one was Maylands, near Romford, which handled scheduled services from April 1932, and the second was Stapleford from which Hillman's began operations on 1 June 1934. Small wooden buildings served as traffic offices and passenger terminals.

Last of the pre-war London airports which must be mentioned is Gatwick. This was a grass aerodrome beside the London to Brighton railway. It was first used in 1930, but was officially opened as an airport on 6 June 1936 and mainly used by British Airways. Its main claim to fame was its circular terminal building, known as the 'Beehive', and the telescopic covered-ways leading to the aircraft loading positions. The post-war development of Gatwick is described in Chapter 6.

2

Europe's Early Airports

If an airport is defined as a place where passengers arrive or depart in the course of a voyage in an aircraft, then we can be absolutely certain that the very first airports were those commissioned in Germany in 1910 for the handling of passenger flights by hydrogen-filled Zeppelin rigid airships.

The first Zeppelin, the LZ 1, made its maiden flight on 2 July 1900, and the rigid airship had developed sufficiently by November 1909 for the Delag company to be founded to operate passenger flights and undertake Zeppelin crew training.

Zeppelins were built at Friedrichshafen beside Lake Constance (Bodensee) and by June 1910, when the first passenger Zeppelin, the LZ 7 *Deutschland* (*Germany*), was ready for service there were, in addition to the Friedrichshafen shed, a Delag-owned shed at Baden-Baden and a municipal shed at

Düsseldorf. It was from the Düsseldorf shed that passenger flights were due to operate initially and on 28 June 1910 the *Deutschland* set out on its first trip, but unfortunately it crashed.

By the end of 1911 there were sheds at Johannisthal near Berlin and at Gotha; in 1912 sheds were erected at Frankfurt-am-Main and Potsdam; and in the following year there were sheds at Hamburg, Dresden and Leipzig.

In 1913 Delag published a map showing a circular route linking Friedrichshafen, Baden-Baden, Frankfurt, Düsseldorf, Hamburg, Potsdam, Leipzig and Gotha. Projected routes were shown to serve Stuttgart, Emden, Bremen, Brunswick, Dresden and Munich, and it was indicated that at each of these cities an airship shed was under construction.

In fact Delag never operated any regular scheduled

◀ The terminal area of Le Bourget Airport, Paris, in 1931. The passenger terminal is almost in the centre of the photograph, between the two rows of hangars. The largest aircraft is the Handley Page H.P.42 *Hanno*.

services before the 1914–18 war but its seven Zeppelins did carry 33,722 passengers and crew during the course of 1,588 flights.

The Zeppelin harbours, as they were known, consisted of large open areas where the airships could be safely manoeuvred and, normally, a single shed known as a Luftschiffhalle (airship hall). Most of the early sheds could only accommodate one airship but later ones were up to 60 m (196 ft) wide and could house two airships side by side. The sheds had to be long enough to take Zeppelins of up to 150 m (492 ft) in length and with a diameter as great as 14·5 m (47 ft 7 in).

All the Zeppelin harbours were served by rail links and had hydrogen supplies. The sheds contained passenger waiting rooms, and embarkation and disembarkation normally took place within the sheds. The early sheds had outward opening double doors at each end but sliding doors were introduced later. During 1911 or 1912 the Baden-Baden shed is known to have borne the words 'Luftschiffhalle Baden-Baden' in large capital letters along the lower part of its roof.

The Zeppelin harbours at Friedrichshafen and Berlin were used in the latter part of 1919 when the airship LZ 120 *Bodensee* operated scheduled services between those points; and Friedrichshafen and, later, Frankfurt were used as Zeppelin stations between 1928 and 1937 when the LZ 127 *Graf Zeppelin* and LZ 129 *Hindenburg* were operating North and South Atlantic services.

The Zeppelin harbours, or airship stations, did not play a major rôle in air transport, but they were the first airports designed for passenger flights and it was from some of them that the world's first trans-ocean air services were operated.

When commercial air transport began to develop after the 1914–18 war, most of continental Europe's first airports were military aerodromes on which simple facilities were introduced for the handling of commercial traffic. Within a very short time there was a large number of airports throughout Europe, all similar in character and consisting of grass landing areas, a few hangars and a small passenger terminal. There was very little flying outside daylight hours, so most did not have any lighting aids. Landing areas measured only a few hundred metres and 1,000 m (3,280 ft) was exceptional.

Many of these airports have long since disappeared and even the communities they served no longer have air services; but a number of the original airports have been constantly expanded and improved and are still major airports. Le Bourget, northeast of Paris; Schiphol at Amsterdam; Fuhlsbüttel, Hamburg; and Cointrin, Geneva, are all examples of present-day airports developed from the grass aerodromes which originally served those cities. In most places, however, airports have been built on new sites.

Le Bourget was one of the important European airports. It served the needs of the French capital until the war, and has continued to rank as a major international airport to the present day although it is nearing the end of its existence in this rôle. The airport was an odd shape, almost triangular, with Route Nationale No. 2 running along its eastern boundary from southwest to northeast. On the opposite side was the military area and its northern boundary was the south bank of the Morée stream. Civil aircraft hangars and a small passenger terminal were on the eastern boundary. Part of the landing area was unsuitable for use and the longest run provided was about 1,500 m (4,920 ft). When night flying became normal, Le Bourget was well equipped with lighting aids, including an illuminated wind direction indicator, wind strength indicators and a Greek cross which was used to signal permission to land to a particular aircraft and warn others not to land. It is interesting to note that in foggy weather a twenty minute interval was enforced between take-offs. It was at Le Bourget, in May 1927, that Charles Lindbergh landed his Ryan monoplane *Spirit of St. Louis* at the end of the first solo crossing of the North Atlantic and the first nonstop flight between the continents of North America and Europe. In 1937 a very large terminal building was opened and it was probably the finest in use in Europe before the war and still forms part of the present facilities.

Near Marseilles there was the combined land-and-marine airport of Marignane. This comprised a grass landing area measuring about 1,000 m (3,280 ft) square and the necessary terminal buildings and hangars. The landing ground became soft after rain and red pennants had to be used to mark the dangerous areas. At the northern end of the airport, on the Étang de Berre, were facilities for flying-boats, including a 10-ton crane for hoisting them out of the water.

An airport that played a most important part in the development of French long-distance air transport was Francazal at Toulouse. This was a grass aerodrome providing take-off and landing runs of about 600 m (1,968 ft) and it was from this airport that the pioneer West Africa and South America mail services were operated by fleets of Breguet biplanes and Latécoère monoplanes of the Latécoère Line and Aéropostale.

One of the world's best known airports has for many years been Amsterdam's Schiphol, which is situated about 8 km (5 miles) southwest of the city centre and has an elevation of 4 m (13 ft) *below* sea

Schiphol Airport, Amsterdam, as it was in 1925.

level. There can be few airports built on the site of a naval battle, but Schiphol is certainly one because much of the airport area was reclaimed from the Haarlem Lake on which the ships of the Prince of Orange fought the Spanish fleet in May 1573. In more recent times the lake was drained and became the Haarlemmermeer polder, an area of about 18,000 hectares (45,000 acres) of pasture-land. Schiphol, whose name means 'hole of the ships', occupies the northeast corner of the polder.

The aerodrome was prepared in 1917 for the Netherlands air force and three years later KLM Royal Dutch Airlines began its services from there. Schiphol at that time was a grass square, frequently muddy, measuring roughly 800 by 900 m (2,625 by 2,950 ft) and providing a maximum take-off run of about 1,060 m (3,300 ft). There were half a dozen wooden sheds in one corner.

Schiphol was continuously enlarged and improved to meet the increasing air traffic and it was the second airport in Europe to have paved runways. The fact that the airport was low-lying and frequently wet meant that its landing surface was constantly torn up by the steel shoes of the aircraft tailskids, and as aircraft became much heavier it was obvious that something more substantial than grass was required. Four paved runways were built, then allowing take-offs and landings into eight wind directions. The longest runway, northeast–southwest, was 1,020 m (3,325 ft) and the shortest, southeast–northwest, 750 m (2,460 ft).

Before the 1939–45 war Schiphol was an important air traffic junction, but when Germany invaded the Netherlands in May 1940 the airport suffered considerable damage. However, after the war it was to rise again as a major international airport, and is still the principal airport for the Netherlands and the main base of KLM.

During the early years of Schiphol the airport faced serious competition from Rotterdam's Waalhaven Airport which, from its opening in 1921, had radio and lighting for night operations – amenities not enjoyed by Schiphol until 1926, but Waalhaven's landing area of 750 by 900 m (2,460 by 2,950 ft) could not be enlarged and the airport was right alongside the docks where cranes and ships' masts were serious obstructions.

Belgium's main airport, known alternatively as Evere and Haren, was about 6 km (3¾ miles) northeast of Brussels and had a landing area measuring about 1,000 by 850 m (3,280 by 2,790 ft). It had no particularly outstanding features and has been replaced by a new airport which is very slightly further north.

During the 1920s and 1930s Germany probably operated more domestic air routes than any other

The terminal building, loading apron and taxiways at
Berlin's Tempelhof Airport towards the end of the 1920s.

country, except the United States, and had a very
large number of airports of varying standards and
importance. Berlin was the focal point of Europe's
air transport system at that time and its Tempelhof
Airport was one of the best known and one of the
busiest. It was also one of the most convenient airports, being only 3 km (1·8 miles) south of the centre
of Berlin, having a tram stop outside the entrance

and an underground railway station only 750 m
(800 yards) away.

Tempelhof's landing area measured 1,350 by
1,000 m (4,430 by 3,280 ft) and on the northern
boundary there was a large rectangular terminal
building flanked by hangars. There was a large hard
surfaced loading apron, and paved taxiways led to
the take-off and landing area. For its time Tempel-

hof was well equipped with radio aids and lighting for night and bad weather operation, although its two tall radio masts in the terminal area were among its least attractive features. Shortly before the war, work began on an ambitious expansion and modernisation scheme. The landing area was considerably increased and the airport became almost circular in shape. To occupy almost a quarter of the boundary a massive terminal building was designed, with a continuous cantilever roof beneath which the aircraft were to park for loading and unloading. Equally massive buildings, in true Third Reich style, were to form the entrance complex between the road and the curved terminal. This grandiose terminal (in plan it represented an eagle with wings spread) was built although it was not entirely completed before the war; but much of the original terminal area was still in existence after the war. Tempelhof, with parallel runways giving a maximum take-off length of 2,115 m (6,942 ft), is still the main airport serving West Berlin, although it is completely surrounded by built-up areas and the landing approaches are made *beside* tall blocks of flats.

In the last few years before the war Germany began to modernise many of its airports and constructed some quite attractive simple terminal buildings such as that at Frankfurt-am-Main which became a combined airport for aeroplanes and Zeppelins. Many of the airport terminals were badly damaged by bombing during the war but were repaired to serve as the post-war first generation of passenger facilities.

Switzerland's most important pre-war airports were Cointrin, Geneva, and Dübendorf, Zürich. Cointrin, 3·5 km (2¼ miles) northwest of the city was a grass field with a landing area measuring 1,000 by 500 m (3,280 by 1,640 ft), and Dübendorf, east-northeast of Zürich, had a grass landing area of 1,200 by 800 m (3,940 by 2,625 ft). The Geneva airport, at an elevation of 422 m (1,384 ft), has been steadily developed and still serves as Geneva's international airport, but Dübendorf, 440 m (1,443 ft) above sea level, has been replaced by a completely new airport. Basle and Bern airports have also played an important part in Swiss commercial aviation.

In Scandinavia, because of the terrain, construction of airports was extremely difficult except in Denmark and southern Sweden, and for many years Norway, Sweden, and Finland operated much of their air transport with twin-float seaplanes, some of which, in the winter, were fitted with skis.

Almost from the beginning of air transport in Denmark, Kastrup has been the country's main airport. Situated on the coast just to the southeast of Copenhagen, Kastrup for many years comprised a grass landing area measuring 900 by 750 m (2,950

Kastrup Airport, Copenhagen, in the mid-1930s. The terminal building is near the centre of the photograph and at the top left can be seen the seaplane jetty.

by 2,460 ft), a small terminal and a number of hangars. Copenhagen has long been an extremely important air traffic junction and, much enlarged, Kastrup still serves as Denmark's international airport.

Bulltofta, the small grass aerodrome 3·5 km (2¼ miles) east of Malmö, was for several years Sweden's terminal for services operated by landplanes. It was not until May 1936, when Bromma was opened, that Stockholm had a land airport. Four paved runways (the first in Europe), each originally about 1,000 m (3,280 ft) long, were blasted out of the rock, and an attractive terminal and large hangar completed what was then one of Europe's best airports. Considerable extension has since taken place and Bromma now serves as Stockholm's secondary airport, handling domestic services.

Similar airports were constructed to provide Helsinki, the Finnish capital, with an all-weather land airport – Malmi opened in 1936 – and to provide Oslo with a much needed airport, at Fornebu. Malmi has been replaced by a new Helsinki Airport but in spite of the difficult site Oslo's Fornebu has been considerably extended and remains in service.

In Italy, there was a number of early airports in the north of the country, but it was only after the Second World War that Rome was to become one of the most important air transport centres in Europe and a port of call for many of the services linking Europe with Africa and the East. Before the war most air services to and from Rome were operated by flying-boats which flew from the waters of the Tiber near Ostia close to the present Leonardo da Vinci Airport. There was, however, a small airport, Littorio, also known as Urbe, situated inside a loop in the Tiber north of the city. This provided a maximum take-off run of about 1,000 m (3,280 ft) and had an unusual double-deck hangar with an inclined ramp leading to the upper level.

In addition to the pre-war airports described, there

were scores of others throughout the continent but this chapter presents a brief glimpse of the more important, as a background to the present system of airports described later.

Bromma Airport, Stockholm, with its original runway pattern.
The airport was opened in May 1936.

3

Along the Trunk Routes

In order to understand how the worldwide system of airports came into being it is necessary to study the development of some of the great trunk air routes. When commercial air transport began after the 1914–18 war, Britain began planning an extensive system of air routes linking the United Kingdom with British territories throughout the world; France embarked on one of the greatest feats in air transport – a mail service between France and South America, as well as a route to the Far East; the Netherlands planned a route to the East Indies, now Indonesia; and Belgium pioneered an air route to the Belgian Congo, now Zaire.

The problems facing all these European countries were similar and centred on the short range, limited performance and poor payload of the aircraft of the period and the complete lack of aerodromes and

facilities along the chosen routes.

The British efforts were typical and can serve to illustrate the problems and how they were overcome.

The first aim of the British Government was the establishment of a trunk airline route from the United Kingdom to India with the intention of ultimately extending it to Australia, and, after opening the India service, to link the United Kingdom and South Africa via the intermediate British territories – then Uganda, Kenya, Tanganyika, and Northern and Southern Rhodesia.

These routes stretched for thousands of miles across all kinds of terrain and involved operating in a very wide range of climates. Deserts, seas, jungles and mountain ranges had to be crossed, aerodromes had to be established at elevations of up to 6,000 ft (1,800 m) or more, and in many places where shade

◀ The landing ground at Bahrein in 1934, with the Imperial Airways Handley Page H.P.42 *Hannibal* being fuelled. Today Bahrein has a modern airport with long paved runway.

temperatures frequently exceeded 100 degrees Fahrenheit (37·8 degrees Centigrade). Sandstorms, monsoon cloud and rain, and tropical thunderstorms added to the problems of establishing airlines and even the ants did their best to obstruct by creating great mounds on the landing areas.

The high elevation of some aerodromes and the high temperatures reduced the already modest performance of the aircraft, increased their take-off runs, reduced their operating heights and cut down their payloads and safe operating range.

The short range meant that aerodromes had to be constructed every few hundred miles so that aircraft could refuel, and the low speed made night stop facilities necessary at frequent intervals. In addition, the comparatively unreliable engines of that period made it advisable, if not essential, to provide emergency landing grounds between the aerodromes at which scheduled calls were made. Strong headwinds could greatly reduce the stages flown – sometimes less than 200 miles (320 km).

The first stage of the original British trunk route came into being through political and military necessity. In Cairo in March 1920 it was proposed by the British Chief of the Air Staff, Sir Hugh Trenchard, that air forces should be used in place of ground forces for the policing of Mesopotamia (now Iraq), and the adoption of this proposal led to the estab-

lishment of the Desert Air Mail, now famous as the Baghdad Air Mail.

The decision was taken to run a mail service between Cairo and Baghdad and this involved a long desert crossing of about 500 miles (nearly 800 km) between Amman and Baghdad and surmounting high mountains in what was then Palestine. There was a military aerodrome at Heliopolis on the outskirts of Cairo, further military aerodromes existed in Palestine and Trans-Jordan, there was an air force station at Ramadi west of Baghdad, and soon after the mail service opened, in June 1921, the RAF station at Hinaidi, just south of Baghdad, served as the eastern terminal. The desert has an average elevation of 2,000 ft (600 m) above sea level and is subject to very high daytime temperatures although it can be very cold at night.

Landing grounds were marked out at intervals of 15 to 30 miles (25 to 50 km) and a furrow was ploughed between the landing grounds of some sectors to act as a navigational aid. The landing grounds were marked A to R, but omitting I and Q, from the west, and over the eastern part of the route they were numbered I to X from the east but with an Arabic numeral being used for landing ground 8. Fuel was provided at Landing Grounds D and V (L.G.D. and L.G.V). Scattered throughout the desert are many large mud flats and their baked surfaces made ideal landing grounds when dry but sudden rain could turn them into lakes. A major problem was camelthorn which could and did puncture the aircraft tyres.

Single-engined de Havilland 9As and twin-engined Vickers Vimys, Vernons and Victorias were used to fly the mail. Much was learned about flying under these conditions, and the disadvantages of water-cooled engines were amply demonstrated, but the service achieved a fine record and there were occasions when the entire journey was made in one day.

In January 1927 Imperial Airways opened Britain's first commercial trunk overseas service when it took over the RAF's Cairo–Baghdad service and extended it to Basra. The aircraft used were specially designed de Havilland 66 Hercules biplanes, each with three Bristol Jupiter air-cooled engines which were more suitable for the high temperatures encountered. Gaza, then in Palestine, was an intermediate stop, and a fort, resthouse and fuel supply was provided at Rutbah Wells in the Syrian Desert.

Political and technical difficulties prevented operation of the England–Egypt link and the extension to India until the end of March 1929 when the London–Karachi service was opened. At that time the sector between Basle, in Switzerland, and Genoa, in northern Italy, was covered by train, and Short Calcutta flying-boats worked between Genoa and Alexandria. Various routes across Europe were tried by Argosy landplanes but poor aerodromes, difficult terrain and weather, limited aircraft performance and political problems prevented successful operation and for most of the time, until flying-boats worked the whole route from England, the India and Africa routes involved a railway sector between France or Switzerland and Italy.

When the India route was opened, beyond Basra the services worked via Bushire, Lingeh and Jask, all in Persia, and Gwadar, in Baluchistan, to Karachi. All the landing grounds were on stony desert and even the Karachi airport was in the desert to the east of the town. In October 1932 the route was changed to the Arabian side of the Gulf with stops at Kuwait, Bahrein and Sharjah before crossing the sea to Gwadar. The new aerodromes were again areas of desert with the minimum of facilities but at Sharjah there was a fort and resthouse similar to that at Rutbah Wells, and an armed guard was provided to protect the passengers.

Early in 1931 Imperial Airways opened the first stages of the much more difficult route through Africa. The ground slopes gradually from sea level in northern Egypt to about 4,000 ft (1,200 m) around Lake Victoria and to a peak of nearly 6,000

The Handley Page H.P.42 *Hanno* on the landing ground at Sharjah in the mid-1930s. The fort/resthouse is in the background and the armed guard and defensive wire in the foreground.

ft (1,800 m) at Johannesburg. The northern part of the route follows the Nile and crosses the great deserts of Egypt and Sudan, then it traverses the Sudd swamps of southern Sudan before reaching tropical Africa with its great lake system.

Desert landing grounds were provided as far south as Khartoum but the difficulty of providing aerodromes further south led to the use of flying-boats from Khartoum to Mwanza at the southern end of Lake Victoria – the original terminal. How-ever, by the end of 1932 aerodromes had been established throughout the length of Africa and landplanes were working regular services all the way from Cairo to Cape Town.

Passenger resthouses were built at some places, hangars and workshops were provided at key aerodromes, and radio stations were erected. Initially, flying was mostly confined to daylight but, later, landing floodlights and flare paths were brought into use to speed up the schedules.

In the east the India route was extended in stages across India, Burma, Thailand and Malaya to Singapore and by the end of 1934 the entire route was open to Australia.

On both the African and the eastern route the aerodromes were subjected to extreme weather variations. In the dry seasons the aircraft took-off leaving mile-long trails of dust behind them, so dry were the aerodrome surfaces, but in the wet seasons aerodromes were frequently flooded and aircraft were often bogged down in deep mud, for there were no paved runways along routes before the 1939–45 war. In fact most of the aerodromes were primitive, although terminal buildings were erected at Baghdad West, Basra (Margil), Karachi and Delhi on the eastern route and at Johannesburg on the African route.

For more than a decade, until the loss of the R 101 in 1930, it was thought that big rigid airships would be used to provide the trunk air services, and Karachi airport actually had a tall mooring mast and a massive airship shed which was not dismantled until the 1960s. The best airport on the eastern route was almost certainly the combined land-and-marine airport which was opened at Singapore in June 1937. This had a smooth grass landing area, modern terminal building, maintenance hangars, and slipways for flying-boats.

When the air route was extended from Singapore to Brisbane in Queensland, aerodromes were prepared across Australia and these were spaced at intervals of 50 to 200 miles (80 to 320 km) from Darwin to Brisbane. Most were primitive landing areas but a few had a hangar and small passenger buildings.

Extensions of the eastern route to Hongkong and the African route from Khartoum to West Africa brought more aerodromes into being but these were of similar nature – desert strips or clearings in the bush.

The French, Belgian and Dutch services were operated through aerodromes similar to those used by the British and on the eastern route British,

The airship shed and mooring mast at Karachi.

French and Dutch services frequently used the same aerodromes.

On the French air mail route to West Africa and South America the aerodromes were similar to those used elsewhere. Desert landing grounds served the mail aircraft on the African coast and Villa Cisneros in Rio de Oro bore a resemblance to the Rutbah and Sharjah landing grounds used by Imperial Airways.

The other great pioneering air route ventures were those of Lufthansa across the South Atlantic and Pan American Airways from the United States to South America and, later, across the Pacific, but all these operations were undertaken by flying-boats and did not require land aerodromes. The facilities provided for the flying-boats are described in the Marine Airports chapter.

On the British routes flying-boats took over the main operations in the late 1930s and there was therefore little development of the airports until the changed situation of war led to the construction of military all-weather airports which were destined to serve the air routes in the post-war years.

Singapore combined land-and-marine airport which was opened in June 1937.

4

The Modern Airport

It is difficult to define the term modern airport because air transport's rate of development is so rapid that facilities which are regarded as modern when designed or implemented quickly become inadequate and outdated. It is perhaps best simply to say that a modern airport is one which adequately serves all the existent requirements of air transport and the community while at the same time having development potential so that it remains adequate for some years to come.

Many of today's airports are inadequate while others only manage to cope with the demands on them because they have been constantly expanded, with lengthened runways and added or altered buildings.

The reason for this is the fantastically rapid growth of air transport, which was not foreseen. For example the number of passengers carried on scheduled air services in 1950 was 31 million and by 1970 the number had increased ten times to 314 million. These figures are for the world, excluding China and the Soviet Union although it is known that more than 70 million passengers were carried by the Soviet airline Aeroflot in 1970. In the same twenty-one-year period air cargo increased from 730 million tonne-km to 10,810 million – a tonne-km being one metric ton carried one kilometre.

In order to carry this traffic, airline fleets had to be expanded and the aircraft had to be bigger and heavier, with consequent increases in landing and take-off runs. In the ten years 1961–70, the world's airlines, again excluding China and the USSR, increased their fleets from 5,122 to 7,301 aircraft – the number of turbojet-powered aeroplanes rising

from 609 to 3,771.

Immediately after the 1939–45 war the most common transport aeroplane was the Douglas DC-3, which, designed for twenty-one passengers, had a maximum weight of 28,000 lb (12,700 kg) and could operate from aerodromes providing runs of well under 4,000 ft (1,220 m). In the 1950s the main long-distance transport aircraft were the Douglas DC-6 and DC-7 series and the Lockheed Constellations and Super Constellations. These aircraft weighed up to 160,000 lb (72,575 kg), carried 50–90 passengers, and, at sea level, required runways of 6,000–7,000 ft (1,830–2,135 m). Late in 1959 the large intercontinental jet transport began to enter service. This could carry about 150 passengers, weighed well over 300,000 lb (136,000 kg), and needed runways of 10,000 ft (3,050 m) or more according to temperature and elevation. Then in January 1970 the biggest of all commercial transport aeroplanes entered service – this was the Boeing 747 with an average capacity for 360 passengers or 100 tons of cargo. It now has a maximum take-off weight of 775,000 lb (351,500 kg) and requires runways of 10,000–12,000 ft (3,050–3,660 m).

This growth of traffic and consequent increase in size and weight of aircraft illustrates the problems which faced the airport planners.

Before describing the physical requirements of the modern airport, it is necessary to establish the importance of airports and air transport to world communications. The airport has now become a vital part of the economy. For example, in the United Kingdom London's Heathrow Airport is the country's busiest passenger port, handling three times as many people as Dover which is the top-ranking passenger seaport, and Gatwick, Luton, Manchester and Glasgow airports come third, fourth, fifth and sixth before the second busiest seaport, Harwich. In terms of value of trade handled through the ports, the seaports of London and Liverpool occupy the first two places with Heathrow in third position.

The aeroplane has revolutionised travel. Anyone with two weeks annual holiday can now spend it on the opposite side of the globe – provided they can afford the fare – because no two major cities are more than two days apart.

Beirut, Cairo, Rome, Frankfurt, Copenhagen and many other places are important junctions because of the aeroplane. Beirut and Copenhagen certainly are seaports but the volume of traffic handled by these cities would never have reached its present level had it not been for the existence of these cities' airports. In many places air transport has replaced, at least to a large extent, surface transport. In the United States the railway plays only a small part in medium- and long-distance travel and the airport

◄ This 1966 photograph on the approach to runway 13 at LaGuardia Airport, New York, shows a well marked runway, parallel taxiway with turn-offs, and, on the right, the terminal area. The runway distance coding marks are clearly visible.

is of far greater importance than the railway station; in other places the aeroplane has taken over from the camel. Over the North Atlantic the majority of *all* passengers travel by air.

Thus it will be seen that airports are an essential feature of major cities and that they are equally important for many small communities, particularly those not well served by surface transport.

The major airports, handling long- and medium-distance and high-density traffic, have themselves become cities with, in some cases, more than 50,000 inhabitants composed of airport and airline staff.

The airport site must be large, as flat as possible, with unobstructed approaches, and it must be easily accessible to the communities it is designed to serve while at the same time being socially acceptable – that is, not causing a nuisance from excessive noise or pollution.

From an operational point of view the runways must be of sufficient length and strength for the heaviest aircraft using the airport. There may be a single runway, a pair of parallel runways or several single or parallel runways aligned to cater for a multiplicity of wind directions. If the airport is in an area subject to high temperatures, or is situated at a high elevation, its runways will have to be longer than they would at sea level or in a temperate climate because aircraft performance deteriorates with

increases in heat and elevation. Runways should also be longer in places where there is heavy rainfall because take-off and landing runs are increased when the surface is wet.

On average, runways at major airports, at sea level, are about 8,000–12,000 ft (2,440–3,660 m) in length whereas the single runway at Nairobi, in Kenya, at an elevation of 5,327 ft (1,625 m), is 13,507 ft (4,117 m) in length. Most major runways are 150 ft (50 m) or 200 ft (60 m) wide. Runway surfaces vary but, as runways must be designed for long life, most are of concrete and anywhere up to 2 ft (about 60 cm) thick. Hard shoulders are situated alongside the runway in case an aircraft goes off the side, and there are normally clearways and stopways at each end. Although the ideal runway is level, many slope or even have a number of different gradients within their length and this slope has to be taken into account when calculating take-off distances. In order to provide better braking for aircraft landing in wet weather some runways now have transverse grooves in their surfaces.

Runways are given painted markings to assist pilots. At each end is the runway number indicating its magnetic alignment. For example, an east–west runway will have the figures 27 painted on its eastern threshold and 09 or 9 on its western end. These figures are derived from the compass points 270

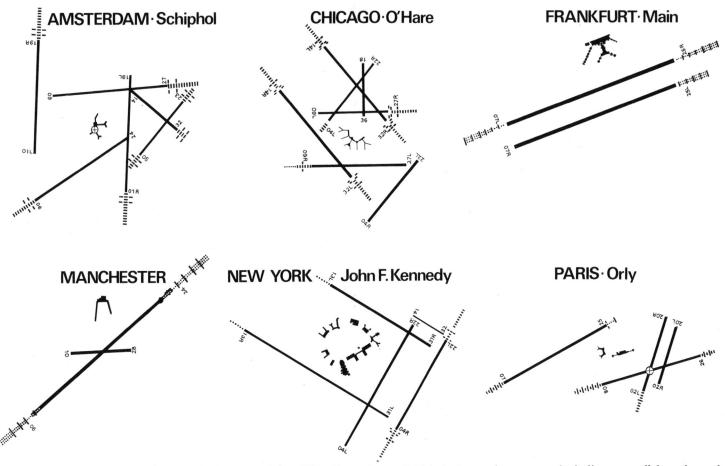

Six examples of runway layouts in use in Europe and the USA. Amsterdam - Schiphol: four main runways, including a parallel north–south pair, and two short runways. A third north–south runway may be added. Chicago - O'Hare: three sets of parallel runways and a limited use north–south runway. Frankfurt - Main: a parallel pair. Manchester: a single main runway. New York - John F. Kennedy International: two parallel pairs. Paris - Orly: a parallel pair and two east–west runways with 10 degrees difference in alignment. For simplicity only runways, runway designations, approach lights and terminal buildings are shown. The drawings are not to the same scale.

degrees for due west and 90 degrees for due east. The runway designation number is associated with the runway threshold, or end, markings which take the form of a series of parallel stripes 30 m (100 ft) long. An instrument or non-instrument approach runway may have its number centred near the threshold, with the stripes on each side of the number; a precision approach runway, and some others, will have a continuous row of threshold stripes or bars and beyond them the runway number; where there are parallel runways the number will be suffixed L for left or R for right. In projected airports with two sets of parallel runways, the inner runways will be designated LC and RC, the C meaning centre as opposed to outer.

In addition to the threshold and designation markings, runways have a centreline and, frequently, a line inset from each edge. Some runways have markings defining the touchdown aiming area and in certain cases these are coded to indicate distance, the zone markings nearest the threshold having four bars each side of the centreline, the next three, the third group two and the final group only one. At some airports indicators beside the runway show the pilot how much runway remains in front of him in which to take-off or bring the aircraft to a halt.

Instrument runways are equipped with instru-

Modern runway and approach lighting. In the foreground is the inner section of the approach centreline and one of the crossbars. The threshold lights cut across the picture and beyond are the runway edge lights and narrow-gauge touchdown zone lights. In the distance can be seen the runway centreline lights, and leading away to the left, the high-speed turn-off taxiway lights.

ment landing systems (ILS) which transmit radio beams along the aircraft's approach path to indicate the correct heading and glidepath to the runway threshold. Using ILS the pilot follows the indications on his instruments, or the ILS can be coupled to the autopilot with the pilot taking control at low altitude. In its most refined form ILS is used to achieve completely automatic landings with the crew monitoring the system.

To a very large extent safe operation at night or in poor visibility is dependent on runway and approach lighting. An airport lighting installation must provide guidance along the runways and taxiways and, most important of all, provide the pilot with ample reference for making a safe landing approach to the runway. Here a description of lighting must be confined to that installed on the approach and the runway.

All runways intended for night use should have white lights along each edge at intervals of not more than 100 m (330 ft) or 60 m (200 ft) if the runway is used for instrument approaches. There should also be green threshold lights across the nearest end of the runway as viewed from an approaching aircraft and red lights across the far threshold. This is really runway lighting at its simplest.

It is now necessary to define the new landing categories which govern the more advanced lighting systems.

ICAO Category I, frequently referred to as Cat I, allows landings with 60 m (200 ft) cloudbase and 800 m ($\frac{1}{2}$ mile) runway visual range (RVR). Category II lowers the limit to 30 m (100 ft) and 400 m ($\frac{1}{4}$ mile). Category III does not demand any limit to the height of the cloud and is divided into three parts – IIIA, 200 m (700 ft) RVR, IIIB, 45 m (150 ft), and IIIC, no external visibility. Aircraft and runways must be certificated for these categories and pilots must have demonstrated their ability to operate to these limits. Operations under Category II are becoming more common and British European Airways Trident 3Bs and the new Lockheed TriStars have been approved for Category IIIA conditions.

All runways used for Category II landings should have centreline lights and they are desirable for Category I. In addition runways for Category II must have touchdown zone lights extending from the threshold for a distance of 900 m (3,000 ft) although the length is reduced on runways of less than 1,800 m (6,000 ft).

For many years one of the best forms of approach lighting has been the Calvert system which consists of a line of lights extending 3,000 ft (900 m) into the approach area from the extended centreline of the runway. These lights, of variable intensity, are coded to show the distance to the runway, the outer third of the line having triple lights, the inner section double lights and the final third single lights. To act as an artificial horizon the Calvert system has six crossbars and these taper towards the threshold to give perspective.

There are many forms of approach lighting including a simplified Calvert with, in some cases, only one crossbar. There are also systems, mainly used in the United States, where lights flash in sequence leading to the runway. Now that weather limits are being further reduced, much more highly developed systems are being introduced for Category II. These include three parallel lines of barrettes with crossbars and in the runway itself touchdown zone lights which are a continuation of the outer approach barrettes.

Also in widescale use are VASI (Visual Approach Slope Indicators) which, by use of a colour code, indicate the correct approach angle to ensure a landing on the correct part of the runway. The VASI system is still being refined to meet changing needs.

Runway layout and variation, lighting and other aids are a fascinating study, but this brief description must suffice for it is necessary to look, even more briefly, at other aspects of an airport.

Taxiways must lead from runways to terminal area,

cargo terminals and maintenance areas and there must be very extensive parking areas (normally known as aprons or ramps) for aircraft. Some of the worst congestion at airports has been caused by insufficient ramp space.

The variations on terminal design are enormous but the basic aim is to construct a terminal building which involves the shortest possible distance between the roadside kerb and the aircraft. Between these points must be baggage and ticket check-in areas, immigration and customs facilities and waiting areas. The terminal should separate departing and arriving traffic and provide for airline offices, restaurants, bars, shops and all other facilities required by passengers and staff. Many airports have piers or traffic fingers leading from the terminal to the aircraft (some with moving pavements) and more recently the trend has been towards building satellite terminals at the outer ends of the piers. Even the generally accepted two-level road system for separating arriving and departing traffic is now being changed to three levels, and at airports where there are several terminals work is in hand to develop some kind of transport system to link them. At Washington's Dulles Airport large mobile lounges carry passengers from the terminal to the aircraft, and this system has recently been adopted for some loading positions at New York's John F. Kennedy.

The modern terminal with traffic pier containing lounge and boarding-gate positions. This is part of the new LaGuardia terminal. The main building is at top left, two of the hangars at top right, and the control tower is centred on the pier.

Cargo terminals are now a feature of the major airports and many of these are becoming terminal cities in their own right with separate terminals for individual airlines – most of them fully automated. At Heathrow there is even a customs bonded tunnel leading from the passenger terminal area beneath the runways to the cargo terminals.

Every major airport has its control tower with a commanding view of the entire airport, but since the advent of radar many air traffic control centres have been moved away from the airports to sites where the land is less valuable.

Hangars and workshops are features of major airports and some of the hangars are truly vast – holding several of the largest types of aircraft.

Fire and rescue services must be provided at all airports as well as large-capacity fuel tank farms and fleets of large refuellers capable of servicing the biggest aircraft in a matter of minutes.

A major problem is providing space for car parking – cars take up an enormous area and at some airports multi-storey car parks have had to be built.

Airport access also presents a major problem. Buses and private cars are the most commonly used vehicles between cities and airports, although a few airports, including Brussels and London Gatwick, are served directly by train. Helicopters are used to some extent but they are too expensive to operate and too small. Increasing congestion on the roads, almost everywhere, is making the journey to the airport more and more frustrating and to some extent negating the speed advantage of the aeroplane. Some way must be found of speeding up the city to airport journey and much thought is being given to such systems as monorail and tracked hovercraft.

5

New York and the USA

The United States is a vast country with a population of more than two hundred million people and its air transport system carries well over half of the entire world's air traffic, if we exclude that in the Soviet Union. This US traffic is generated by widely differing types of air service: there are several very large major trunk route airlines such as American Airlines, Eastern Air Lines and United Air Lines, which have wide-ranging networks of services including nonstop coast-to-coast and services linking the New York/Boston/Washington area with the Middle West and Florida – these three airlines alone carry about seventy million passengers a year; there are the somewhat smaller trunk airlines such as Braniff, Continental, Delta, National and Northwest; the local service airlines – now becoming quite big – which provide networks of regional services;

commuter or third level airlines which fit in between the local service airlines and the many air taxi companies; and there are the helicopter airlines, the charter companies and the all-cargo airlines. In addition there are the international operations of big carriers including Pan American World Airways and TWA, the latter also having an extensive domestic network. Added to the traffic of all these American airlines is that picked up and set down in the United States by the airlines of other countries.

To handle this enormous traffic the United States has a great many airports which range in size, complexity and equipment from the major airports serving New York, Chicago, Washington, Los Angeles, Dallas, Miami and Boston, down to small grass fields which may have no more facilities than a small passenger building and the Government

◀ This view of Newark Airport, taken in August 1971, shows the new terminal area under construction. Two of the terminal buildings, each with three satellites, are far advanced. The outline of the third terminal can be seen in the foreground.

required fire and rescue services.

In view of the very large number of airports – by 1931 there were 644 municipal airports and 663 other commercial airports – in the United States, it is not possible to describe all of even the most important, and therefore, following a brief historical review, the New York/New Jersey airports are described at some length as representative of the way in which the United States airports have developed.

Rather strangely, organised commercial air transport in the USA did not come into being as early as it did in Europe although the world's first scheduled passenger air service was in fact operated in the United States. This began in Florida in 1914 and was worked by flying-boats, and after the First World War a number of short-lived services were also operated with flying-boats. By far the biggest air transport undertaking in the United States in 1919 and the early 1920s was the establishment of the transcontinental air mail service.

The transcontinental mail service was an outstanding achievement and involved setting up a chain of aerodromes stretching from coast to coast. The mail services were operated by the US Post Office, mainly with a fleet of single-engined DH-4 biplanes with open cockpits. A Washington–New York mail service began in May 1918 and then in May 1919 a Cleveland–Chicago service was inaug-

urated as the first stage of the transcontinental route. By the end of that July the entire New York–Chicago sector was in operation as well as the first western stretch, between San Francisco and Sacramento. The Chicago–Omaha sector was opened in May 1920, and that September the difficult sector across the Rocky Mountains was opened to provide the Sacramento–Omaha link and the entire route was in being. Initially, flying was confined to daylight but by the end of 1923 a lighted airway had been established between Chicago and Cheyenne in Wyoming, two years later the lighted airway extended from New York to Salt Lake City, and in 1927 it was completed to the West Coast, from Chicago to Dallas and from Boston through New York to Atlanta.

To operate the mail services, aerodromes were established right across the country, with emergency landing grounds between the regular stops. At most places cinder runways were laid out and rolled into the aerodrome surface. There were normally two runways, at right angles, which measured about 2,000 to 2,500 ft (610 to 760 m) in length and were 250 ft (76 m) wide. Hangars were erected at the main aerodromes. At all the regular stops there was a 500,000 candle-power revolving beacon mounted on a 50-ft (15 m) tower – this revolved every twenty seconds and in good weather could be seen more than 100 miles (160 km) away. At the emergency landing grounds there were 50,000 candle-power revolving beacons. White lights outlined the landing areas, there were red lights on all the obstructions and at the regular aerodromes there were floodlights to illuminate the landing area. In addition there were acetylene-gas beacons every 3 miles (5 km) along the route to assist the pilots' navigation.

In 1927 the Post Office turned over its transcontinental mail route to private operators. Boeing Air Transport operated the San Francisco–Chicago sector and National Air Transport provided the Chicago–New York link. The Boeing aircraft could each carry two passengers, in some discomfort, but passengers were not welcomed on NAT's services.

Another transcontinental service was opened in July 1929. This was operated by Transcontinental Air Transport with Ford Tri-motors and involved flying during daylight and travelling by train at night. Passengers journeying westward set out by train from Pennsylvania Station in New York and arrived in the early morning at Port Columbus in Ohio where they transferred to the Ford Tri-motor. This interchange was made at a specially constructed airport beside the railway. There was an airport terminal building and from it a covered walkway led directly to the railway station platforms. A change back to train was made at Waynoka in

Oklahoma, and the final sector, from Clovis, New Mexico, to Los Angeles, was by air. The entire journey took two days and nights.

The combined rail-air operation was not the most successful method of crossing the continent and the subsequent history of the route has been a continual development with steadily reduced journey times, and, over the past twenty years, regular nonstop services.

Numerous aerodromes in the New York area have been used for the operation of air services, with some acting as the eastern terminal for transcontinental flights, but three have played a major rôle and these form the New York/New Jersey airport complex which now handles about 850,000 aircraft movements, nearly forty million passengers and more than a million tons of cargo annually. These airports are John F. Kennedy International, LaGuardia and Newark.

The story starts with Newark. Situated in New Jersey in the southern part of the City of Newark and adjacent to Elizabeth, this airport was opened on 1 October 1928 and at that time occupied an area of 68 acres (28 hectares). Originally known as Newark Metropolitan Airport, it had a 1,600 ft (490 m) long runway which was claimed to be the first hard-surfaced runway at a United States commercial airport, and this would appear to make it the first of its kind anywhere in the world.* There were several large hangars – that is, large for that period – and by the early 1930s Eastern Air Transport (now Eastern Air Lines) and United Air Lines had erected 'passenger stations' on the landing-ground side of their hangars. The United passenger building was in Southern colonial style with high slender-columned portico. This system of attaching the passenger terminal to the hangar was not uncommon in the United States in the late 1920s and early 1930s, examples being known at Cleveland and Wichita.

Newark was equipped for night flying, and in 1930 handled 28,000 landings and more than 20,000 passengers. By that time it had become one of the six most important airports in the United States.

Over the years Newark was developed to have more and longer runways, the number of hangars was increased, and a building was erected which became the administration centre and later the terminal.

In 1948, the Port of New York Authority took over operation under the terms of a fifty-year lease from the City of Newark, thus eliminating the burden on the taxpayers. At that time the airport occupied 1,400 acres (560 hectares) and had three runways, all unsuitable for the types of aircraft then

about to come into service. The Authority increased the area to 2,300 acres (920 hectares), improved the east–west runway, and replaced the other two by a new 7,000 ft (2,135 m) instrument runway aligned northeast–southwest (04–22). A new taxiway was laid parallel to the runway and seven intersections connected the two. New radar and approach lighting was installed and the runway was specially marked to assist pilots landing in bad visibility. A new passenger terminal was built which at that time was one of the biggest and most modern, and it was designed to become a hangar when it in turn was replaced. New hangars and a cargo terminal were also constructed and a new control tower came into operation in 1959.

The instrument runway was commissioned in November 1952 and the terminal in July 1953 and Newark had been transformed into a modern and extremely useful airport; but air traffic continued to grow at a phenomenal rate and in 1958 the jet transports began to appear in American skies. For several years airline passengers have been doubling in number every five years, although there has been a temporary slowing of the rate over the past two years, and cargo volume has been growing even faster. It was therefore decided that Newark Airport would again have to be redeveloped and the Port Authority embarked on an ambitious programme which it is

* This Newark claim has been widely reported but there is evidence that in 1925 the Ford Airport at Dearborn had two concrete runways, of 2,600 and 2,800 ft. (792 and 853 m).

estimated will cost more than $400 million.

The initial steps involved filling a large area of meadowland south. of the east–west runway, in order to build a completely new terminal area, and construction of a second main runway. The new runway, designated 4L–22R, was built 950 ft (290 m) to the west of the earlier instrument runway, now redesignated 4R–22L, and is 8,200 ft (2,500 m) long. It is equipped with centreline and edge lights, has ILS at each end and approach lights leading to its southern end. The older instrument runway has been increased in length to 9,800 ft (3,000 m), it has centreline, edge and touchdown zone lights, and ILS and approach lights at each end. The secondary runway, 11–29, the old east–west runway, has been lengthened to 7,300 ft (2,225 m) but is only used by transport aircraft when the other runways are subjected to excessive crosswinds.

The major undertaking at Newark, which is transforming it into virtually a new airport, is the terminal area. Three large curved buildings, all served by three-level roads, each have three circular satellite terminals. The main terminals are connected to the satellites by elevated covered arcades and eventually will be connected with each other and with carparks and heliport by some form of automatic transport system. Each of the three main terminals is about 800 ft (245 m) long and 165 ft (50 m)

deep and the satellites are approximately 200 ft (60 m) in diameter. Aircraft will be parked nose-in to the satellites; in the final plan there will be 83 aircraft loading positions; and the terminals have been designed to handle more than 12 million passengers a year. There is parking space for 10,000 cars and the roads for departing and arriving passengers have been kept at separate levels with a third, lower, level providing access for close-in parking. By the end of 1971 the shells of the first two terminals were almost complete and much of the steel structure of the third terminal was in place.

It must be regarded as a significant achievement to more than double the capacity of the airport while at the same time keeping it in full operation.

Among the New Yorkers who in the 1930s did not think it right that their city should be served only by an airport in New Jersey was Mayor Fiorello LaGuardia and it was he who was most responsible for the city government decision to build its own airport in Long Island, on the borders of Flushing and Bowery Bays only 8 miles (12 km) from 42nd Street in the heart of Manhattan.

On this Long Island site, at North Beach, had been the Gala Amusement Park, but in 1929 an area of 105 acres (42 hectares) had been developed as the Glenn H. Curtiss Airport for private flying. The City of New York acquired this rather primitive air-

port in 1935 and increased its area to 558 acres (220 hectares), partly by buying extra land but mainly by filling in at the edge of the Bays – a process which was later to cause considerable difficulty for the city and its airport.

Under the title New York Municipal Airport-LaGuardia Field, the airport was opened to commercial traffic on 2 December 1939 and it was renamed LaGuardia Airport in 1947. Four runways were built and on the land side, constructed in a large sweeping curve, were the terminal building and on either side a row of hangars. A covered arcade between the terminal and the hangars gave access to the aircraft loading areas and provided an elevated observation deck. The control tower was mounted on top of the terminal building, which comprised a circular building projecting from a three-storey rectangular structure.

LaGuardia suffered a number of problems. Spring tides used to inundate the landing area and hangars, and the filling on which much of the airport was built was subject to subsidence to a very marked degree – so serious was this subsidence that the buildings had to be jacked up in an effort to keep them reasonably level. It is said that on one occasion somebody watched a lamp standard sink out of sight!

The Port of New York Authority took over opera-tion of LaGuardia in June 1947 at which time the airport was handling about 145,000 aircraft movements and 2½ million passengers a year. This traffic increased rapidly until it was considered that it exceeded the safe capacity of the airport and this, combined with the previously mentioned problems, led the Port Authority to undertake the formidable task of rebuilding the airport and at the same time keeping it in operation with as little disruption as possible.

The old terminal was demolished and in its place was built a fine curved terminal building which is four-storeys high in the centre and has two three-storey wings. The building is 1,300 ft (395 m) long and 125 ft (38 m) deep and provides 650,000 sq ft (60,000 sq m) of floor space. Projecting from this building are four two-level arcades which have a total of 36 aircraft loading-gate positions. Centred on the left-hand arcade is a 150 ft (45 m) high circular control tower. This whole complex, together with its road system and parking space for 5,000 cars was opened in the spring of 1964.

With the opening of the new terminal, LaGuardia had been transformed into an airport with one of the finest passenger terminals anywhere; but there still remained the task of improving runways, taxiways and other operational features. At this time La-Guardia only had two of its runways remaining in

◄ LaGuardia Airport as it was in May 1956. This view shows the airport layout and its proximity to Manhattan, seen in the background. The runway extensions can be seen in the photograph on page 34.

use, the southwest–northeast instrument runway, 04–22, and the southeast–northwest runway, 13–31. Runway 04–22 measured 5,000 ft (1,525 m) in length and 13–31 was 5,965 ft (1,818 m) long. All approaches except that to 04 were over water, and the approach to 04 is over a built-up area so extensions could only be made by building the runways out over the water of Flushing Bay.

In order to lengthen both runways to 7,000 ft (1,820 m) a 50 acre (20 hectare) L-shaped pier had to be built on piles and these pier arms range in width from 700 to 900 ft (215 to 275 m). In the case of the extension to runway 04–22, the entire 2,000 ft (610 m) had to be built out over the water together with taxiways and pre-take-off holding area. Piers, each 3,000 ft (915 m) long, had to be constructed to carry the approach lights to these runways, both of which became fully operational in 1966. These extensions to LaGuardia closed the shipping channel between the airport and Rikers Island, so a new channel 3,200 ft (975 m) long by 400 ft (120 m) wide and 30 ft (9 m) deep had to be dredged to provide a new route.

In addition to the two main runways, LaGuardia now has a 1,600 ft (490 m) runway for light aircraft and a specially marked 835 ft (255 m) STOL runway for short take-off and landing aircraft. These two short runways, which increase the airport's capacity, can only be used during daylight and when VFR (visual flight rules) apply.

LaGuardia is now handling heavy traffic which includes the recently introduced wide-bodied DC-10s, and the airport is a vital part of New York's transport system; but very soon after the original airport was opened it was realised that the city would require a much bigger airport, and a site was selected on the shores of Jamaica Bay about 15 miles (24 km) from the centre of Manhattan. A 1,100 acre (440 hectare) airport was planned and in April 1942 work began on filling the marshy tidelands of the Idlewild golf course. Commercial flying began at the airport on 1 July 1948 and on 31 July that year the airport was officially dedicated as New York International Airport, although to many people it is still known as Idlewild in spite of the fact that in December 1963 it was renamed John F. Kennedy International Airport in memory of the late President.

Work on the international airport was started by the City of New York but in June 1947 the Port of New York Authority became responsible for financing, construction and operation. Kennedy International is truly great and it is hard for anyone to comprehend its size without actually seeing it. The area is just under 5,000 acres (2,000 hectares) and is equivalent to the whole of Manhattan from 42nd

View from 16,500 ft (about 5,000 m) over Jamaica Bay of New York's John F. Kennedy International Airport as it was in October 1959. In the foreground is runway 13R–31L with the parallel 13L–31R beyond the central terminal area. On the right are the parallel 04–22 runways. 04L–22R has now been extended well into the bay.

Street in midtown to the Battery at the seaward tip of the island. Up to 1970 the City of New York and the Port Authority spent well over $500 million on the construction of the airport, and vast sums have also been spent by the airlines on terminals, hangars, workshops and other facilities. In addition it will have cost another $650 million to implement the recent expansion work which is nearing completion – nearly half of this last amount being spent on the central terminal area.

Like London's Heathrow, Kennedy has a central terminal area which is surrounded by runways and taxiways, but the terminal area is vast compared with Heathrow and in it are nine separate terminal buildings. The plans for the airport terminal area were daring and could have proved disastrous but in fact have been both successful and exciting for it is a feast of architectural styles. To the author it is at its most exciting at nightfall when all the lights are on, when aircraft appear as silhouettes and when the distant high buildings of Manhattan can be seen outlined against the pinks and golds of the evening sky.

The original rather ramshackle temporary terminal gave no glimpse of the shape of things to come, but soon the framework of the high control tower and the great curving arch of the Port Authority's International Arrival Building began to dominate the scene.

The International Arrival Building, opened at the end of 1957, was originally 760 ft (230 m) long and 640 ft (195 m) deep and had two double-deck 240 ft (73 m) long fingers, or arcades, leading to the aircraft loading areas. Passengers pass through US

Health, Immigration and Customs on the ground floor of the building. Adjoining the Arrival Building were the two Airline Wing Buildings, each three storeys high, and with arcade extensions leading to the aircraft. These Wing Buildings were designed as departure terminals for non-United States airlines, and the overall length of the three linked buildings was about 1,900 ft (580 m). By the end of 1971 this terminal complex had been enlarged to twice its original size.

Over a period of several years some of the major airlines erected their own terminals. Travelling anti-clockwise round the terminal area from the Port Authority's buildings one comes to the TWA terminal, then those of National Airlines, BOAC, American Airlines and United Air Lines. After crossing the Van Wyck Expressway where it enters the terminal area, there are the Eastern Air Lines terminal, the terminal shared by Braniff and Northwest, and finally the Pan American terminal.

All these terminals were designed specifically to meet the requirements of the individual airlines and most comprise a rectangular building with traffic fingers leading to the aircraft loading positions; but two deserve special mention – the Pan American and TWA terminals.

The Pan American terminal is notable for its roof which is an oval cantilever structure measuring

A recent photograph of the John F. Kennedy terminal area. ▶
The biggest building is the International Arrival Building with its adjoining Airline Wing Buildings. To the right can be seen the large cantilever roof of the Pan American terminal. The parallel 13–31 runways frame the view.

nearly 500 ft (150 m) over its length and nearly 400 ft (120 m) in width. This large canopy, mounted above a rectangular building, allowed aircraft to be parked nose-in to the building so that passengers could embark under cover. But like so many structures built to serve air transport, the Pan American terminal soon proved to be too small, and a very large triangular four-level extension has been constructed with loading-gates for ten aircraft, including six Boeing 747s, to give the overall terminal sixteen loading-gates.

Most dramatic of all the Kennedy terminals is that constructed by TWA. This was designed by the famous architect Eero Saarinen and consists of four intersecting barrel vaults, of varied shapes, supported on columns. It is almost impossible to describe this building in a few words but its overall appearance suggests a great bird and its designer said he intended it to express the excitement of travel and be a place of movement. Originally an enclosed walkway led from this terminal to a single satellite building around which there were seven aircraft loading positions. Now TWA has added a completely new satellite which is bigger than the original terminal. This is known as Flight Wing One and can handle ten Boeing 707s, or four Boeing 747s and three 707s. This terminal is also connected to Saarinen's building by an enclosed walkway.

In addition to the great terminal buildings and control tower, Kennedy has large cargo terminal areas, about a score of large hangars and there are even three chapels beside an ornamental lake.

There are four main runways, a general aviation runway for daylight good weather use, and 20 miles (32 km) of taxiways. The runway pattern has been changed several times during the development of the airport and several runways have been extended. The main runways now comprise two parallel pairs. They are the southeast–northwest pair (13L–31R and 13R–31L) and southwest–northeast (4L–22R and 4R–22L). Runway 13R–31L is the longest at 14,572 ft (4,441 m) and 4R is the main instrument Category II runway, it is 8,400 ft (2,560 m) long and equipped with flush narrow-gauge lights, flush centreline lights, edge lighting and high-intensity approach lights with sequenced flashers.

In 1971 Kennedy International handled 341,814 aircraft movements (nearly 1,000 a day), 19,189,430 passengers and 834,765 tons of cargo. The total number of people working at the airport was more than 41,000 and their salaries totalled about $500 million.

Although the three New York airports handle the biggest volume of traffic in any US city, Chicago's O'Hare Airport handles the biggest volume at a single airport – more than 640,000 aircraft movements and just under 30 million passengers in 1970. This gigantic aircraft movement figure means that on average O'Hare has more than 1,750 take-offs or landings every day of the year.

For many years Midway was the Chicago Airport and after the war it became the world's busiest, but was inadequate to handle the city's traffic. So the private Orchard Place aerodrome was acquired by the city, renamed O'Hare International Airport, and opened to scheduled traffic in 1955. The airport has a large central terminal area and six runways. There are east–west and northwest–southeast parallel pairs, a northeast–southwest runway and a limited-use north–south runway.

The three longest runways are 14R–32L of 11,600 ft (3,371 m), 09R–27L of 10,140 ft (3,090 m) and 14L–32R of 10,000 ft (3,048 m). Runways 14L, 14R, 27R, 32L and 32R all have high-intensity centreline and bar approach lights with sequenced flashers. Runway 09R also has approach lights. The north–south runway, 18–36, is only 5,334 ft (1,625 m) long and its use is restricted to southward landings and northward take-offs because of the proximity of the terminal area. Only single-engined and twin-engined propeller aircraft can land on it if the wind is less than 20 knots (37 km/hr) but with higher wind speeds it can be used by all types except jets. Boeing 747s are allowed to operate only on the 14–32 runways.

After a period of closure, Midway was opened again to airline traffic including jets. It appears that the two airports will have to continue to serve Chicago because the Mayor has rejected proposals for a new offshore airport in Lake Michigan or on any other site.

Lack of space precludes descriptions of other United States airports but in Chapter 17 will be found details of the vast airport now under construction to serve the Dallas/Fort Worth regional area in Texas.

6

Airports of Britain

For most of the war period between 1939 and 1945 no commercial air services were operated into the London area and, in fact, more than half of the wartime domestic air transport was in Scotland; but when commercial air services were resumed, the domestic and European flights used Croydon Airport, and the long-distance services operated to Hurn near Bournemouth on the south coast, and to Prestwick in Scotland.

The first major improvement came early in 1946 when the Royal Air Force station at Northolt was opened for civil operations. This was an old grass aerodrome dating from the 1914–18 war, and during the 1939–45 war it had been a famous fighter station. By 1946 the aerodrome had two paved runways and on its southern boundary a terminal area of prefabricated single-storey buildings was con-

structed. Northolt became the main base of British European Airways and, although by modern standards the airport was small, served civil aviation well until the end of October 1954 when operations were transferred to Heathrow. It was from Northolt that the first passenger services anywhere were flown by a turbine-powered aircraft, when the prototype Vickers Viscount flew to Paris on 29 July 1950. The first domestic turbine-powered service was from Northolt to Edinburgh on 15 August that year.

During the Northolt period other ex-military stations at Blackbushe and Bovingdon were also being used as airports for London.

In the latter part of the war a search had been made for a site near London for an aerodrome for RAF Transport Command. The site chosen was to the west of London and included the old grass aero-

Vertical photograph of London Airport Heathrow before runway 10L–28R was lengthened at its western end (*top left*). The longest runway is 10R–28L, and the crosswind, 05R–23L, runway can be seen to the right of the central terminal area. The BEA and BOAC maintenance complex is on the right and the cargo terminal (*left centre*) to the south of runway 10R–28L.

drome of the Fairey Aviation Company. The design called for the standard RAF pattern of three runways forming a triangle, with the east–west runway being 9,000 ft (2,743 m) long and the southwest–northeast and northwest–southeast runways each having a length of 6,000 ft (1,828 m).

Work on this aerodrome began in 1944, but the war ended before its completion and the decision was taken to make this Heathrow site the major international airport for London. It was decided to double the number of runways by adding another triangle pattern to form three sets of parallel runways, with the terminal area in the centre and the maintenance area in the southeast corner outside the runway pattern. There was also a plan to construct a smaller three-runway system to the north of the Bath Road which runs along the airport's northern boundary, but this was never implemented.

On 1 January 1946 Heathrow was handed over to the civil aviation authorities and on the same day the British South American Airways Avro Lancastrian *Starlight* left the airport on the first British proving flight to South America. The first BOAC service to use Heathrow was that operated by a Lancastrian on 28 May when it left for Australia, and on 31 May the airport was officially opened with TWA and Pan American Lockheed Constellations being the first transatlantic arrivals.

At that time, apart from the first runways, there was a temporary control tower and a terminal area consisting of tents. Airline staff worked in old RAF caravans. Although working conditions were primitive the airport was well equipped with runway and approach lighting and soon acquired a fine reputation for operational efficiency, but for many years it enjoyed an equally bad reputation for its ground services and passenger facilities.

The tented terminal village was soon replaced by a temporary terminal of prefabricated buildings – these were on the north side near the control tower and facing what must by today's standards be regarded as a ludicrously small loading apron.

Work went ahead on the central terminal area and an access road tunnel from the north side which passed under the northern east–west runway and its parallel taxiway. The first central area buildings to come into use were the control block and, on the southeast side of the area, a 620 ft (188 m) long passenger terminal for European and domestic services. This terminal opened on 17 April 1955 and is now known as Terminal 2 – it is used by non-British short-haul airlines, has been considerably expanded and has traffic piers projecting onto the apron. In November 1961 Terminal 3 was brought into use for BOAC services, and all long-haul services used it from March 1962. The northside terminal was then closed for passenger services although retained for cargo flights. The last terminal to be opened at Heathrow was Terminal 1 which was opened by HM the Queen on 17 April 1969. This terminal is mainly used by BEA, and has two long traffic piers with each gate-position served by a telescopic air-jetty, or aero-bridge. Multi-storey carparks occupy a considerable space in the terminal area.

BEA and BOAC have large maintenance areas in the southeast corner of the airport, there is a cargo terminal area on the southern boundary and to the west a fuel tank farm.

Considerable expansion of terminals has taken place at Heathrow and a completely new extension to Terminal 3 was made to handle the Boeing 747s. Work is now in progress to extend the London underground railway system into the airport's central terminal area and there is a possibility that British Rail may link the airport with Victoria Station.

Only three of the original six runways now remain in use. The main runways are 10L–28R of 12,800 ft (3,901 m) and 10R–28L of 12,000 ft (3,657 m). The crosswind runway, 05R–23L, is 7,734 ft (2,357 m) long. All the runways are of concrete, 150 ft (45 m) wide and have precision approach radar. All but 05R have ILS. The total area of Heathrow is 2,721 acres (about 1,008 hectares).

In 1970 Heathrow handled more than 263,000 aircraft movements, 14½ million passengers and 405,000 tons of cargo.

Until 31 March 1966 Heathrow had been the responsibility of the Ministry of Aviation and its predecessors, but on 1 April that year the newly formed British Airports Authority became responsible for ownership and operation of London's Heathrow, Gatwick and Stansted Airports and for Prestwick. Subsequently the Authority took over Edinburgh Airport.

London's second airport, Gatwick, is 28 miles (45 km) south of the city and is served by train from Victoria to the airport's own railway station. It started life as a small grass aerodrome in August 1930 and was opened as a public airport in June 1936. In the mid-1950s a concrete runway, 09–27, was laid and a large new terminal constructed some way to the north of the original site. In its rebuilt form Gatwick was opened by HM the Queen on 9 June 1958 and has been mainly used for short-haul and charter services. It was also for some years BEA's helicopter headquarters – on the site of the old terminal area which is separated, by a road, from the present airport. Originally the Gatwick runway was 7,000 ft (2,133 m) long but this has been extended to 9,075 ft (2,766 m) and, in order to allow nonstop transatlantic flights from the airport, this is to be further extended to a total length of 10,165 ft (3,098 m).

In 1970 Gatwick handled more than 93,000 aircraft movements – more than a third of them being by BAC One-Elevens – and 3,850,000 passengers.

Stansted, to the northeast of London, handles comparatively few scheduled flights but is widely used for air transport training. The airport has a

Gatwick Airport with terminal building, traffic piers, loading aprons and railway station
in the foreground and the runway and taxiways beyond.

10,000 ft (3,048 m) asphalt-surfaced runway, and in 1964 the decision was taken to develop Stansted to become the new major international airport serving London. However, public opposition was so strong that the Government was forced to abandon the idea and look elsewhere.

Also serving the London area are the municipal airports of Luton and Southend. Luton, at an elevation of 520 ft (158 m), has a single 7,087 ft (2,160 m) runway and is used mainly for holiday inclusive tour and charter flights. Southend's longest runway, 06–24, measures 5,265 ft (1,605 m). Part of Southend's traffic consists of vehicle ferry services to and from the continent. It was also this type of traffic which was entirely responsible for the construction of Ferryfield at Lydd close to Dungeness.

Silver City Airways, in July 1948, began a vehicle ferry service, with Bristol Freighters, between Lympne in Kent and Le Touquet in France. Traffic grew to such an extent that the airline required a better main base than the old grass hilltop aerodrome which was at more than 350 ft (106 m) elevation and often affected by bad weather. To overcome these problems Ferryfield was constructed, almost at sea level, and it had a simple terminal and two runways. The airport was opened in July 1954 and on occasions handled more than 200 vehicle flights a day, but eventually all British vehicle ferry services came under the ownership of British Air Ferries and these now work from Southend and Stansted.

There are also airports serving different parts of the United Kingdom. They vary in standard and many are in need of considerable improvement. Manchester's Ringway Airport, opened shortly before the war, has been brought up to jet standards, has a large terminal, and its 9,000 ft (2,743 m) 06–24 runway, with full approach lighting, handles transatlantic services. Speke, Liverpool's airport, also dating from the 1930s has been drastically changed and now has a runway of 7,500 ft (2,286 m).

The main British domestic trunk air routes are those linking London with Belfast, Edinburgh and Glasgow. Belfast has had several airports during the past forty years. That used immediately after the war was Sydenham, close to the harbour, but it had various shortcomings and when larger aircraft were introduced a move was made to Nutts Corner. This in turn gave way to Aldergrove.

All the pioneering of air routes to the Western Isles was based on Glasgow's Renfrew Airport which was originally a grass area. During the war it was provided with two paved runways but the most used approaches were over the cranes of the nearby docks. It was therefore decided to rebuild the Naval Air Station at Abbotsinch and this is now the Glasgow Airport. It has a large terminal building with traffic piers and its 06–24 runway is 7,020 ft (2,140 m) long. Edinburgh's airport, known also as Turnhouse, provides a maximum run of 6,000 ft (1,828 m), but this runway is frequently subjected to strong crosswinds and a plan has now been made for a large-scale redevelopment of the airport.

Scotland's major international airport is Prestwick and this is described in a subsequent chapter as part of the story of the North Atlantic airports.

There is one Scottish 'airport' that deserves special mention. This is on the island of Barra where airport construction proved impossible because of the terrain, and landings and take-offs have to be made on the white cockle beach (tide permitting) which provides a run of 3,000 ft (914 m).

In the early 1930s the beach at St Aubin's Bay served as Jersey's airport, in the Channel Islands, but in 1937 an airport was opened at St Peter and this has been constantly expanded.

Recently small aerodromes such as that at Broad-

ford, in Skye, have been opened to bring air transport to more communities, but the most publicised attempt at providing a new airport has been the search for a new additional London airport. After the rejection of Stansted, further sites were examined and public inquiries held and eventually the Government decided that the new airport should be on an offshore site on the Maplin sands near Foulness on the North Sea coast of Essex. The site would provide four long runways but in many ways is not the most suitable choice. No design details have been released and the airport is unlikely to be operational before the end of the decade.

A really simple 'airport'. The cockle beach landing ground at Barra in Scotland's Outer Hebrides.
The aircraft is a de Havilland Dragon Rapide.

7

Europe Today

In recent years many of Europe's airports have been greatly expanded, some cities have entirely new airports and a number of others have new airports either under construction or in the planning stage.

Paris, served in pre-war years by Le Bourget, has for most of the post-war period been using Orly as well. Now a completely new airport is under construction, with initial operations planned for 1974. The early history of Le Bourget is covered in Chapter 2, and in many ways the airport is essentially as it was except that the terminal has been extended, and there are new hangars and two paved runways with the longest, 07–25, being 3,000 m (9,843 ft). In spite of a gradual transfer of traffic to Orly, Le Bourget handled more than 44,000 commercial aircraft movements and more than two million passengers in 1970, increases of 18 and 26·6 per cent over the previous year.

Orly was an old grass aerodrome to the south of Paris and in pre-war years was distinguished by having two rather attractive arched concrete airship hangars each about 300 m (985 ft) long and 70 m (230 ft) high. Now Orly is the major Paris airport handling nearly 200,000 aircraft movements and more than ten million passengers a year. The runway system has been developed since the war and there are now four, with the longest, 07–25, measuring 3,650 m (11,975 ft). After using several temporary terminals, an impressive permanent building was opened in February 1961 by Général de Gaulle. But traffic continued to grow and in 1969 a west satellite was added to the terminal and an east satellite followed in July 1970. A completely separate terminal, known as Orly-West, was opened in March 1971.

In spite of having two major airports in operation,

Orly Airport, Paris, with the main terminal and its two satellites on the left and Orly-West at the top of the picture.

it was realised that Paris required a much bigger additional airport and construction of this began in December 1966. The new airport, originally known

as Paris Nord and now as Roissy-en-France, is being built 27 km (16¾ miles) northeast of the city and sits astride the A1 motorway to the north. The site occupies 3,000 hectares (about 7,200 acres) and in Phase 1 will have a 3,600 m (11,810 ft) east–west runway, passenger and cargo terminals, maintenance buildings and other essential facilities.

In the final phase, due for completion between 1985 and 1990, there will be two sets of parallel east–west runways, a north-northwest–south-south-east crosswind runway, and a shorter east–west runway for general aviation aircraft. The main pairs of runways will be in the northern and southern areas of the airport, the northern pair being staggered. All five main runways will be 3,600 m (11,810 ft) long and the east–west runways will be capable of extension to 4,000 or even 5,000 m (13,123 or 16,404 ft) if required. There will be an extensive system of taxiways including connections through the centre of the airport to link the north and south runway systems.

There are to be three large eleven-storey circular terminal buildings each with seven satellite buildings round which the aircraft will be parked for loading and unloading. The main terminals will have a diameter of 192 m (630 ft), be 52·7 m (173 ft) high and weigh 300,000 tons. Each satellite will have an area of 2,500 sq m (26,910 sq ft). By 1980 the new

The Roissy-en-France Airport under construction. The first ▶ east–west runway is nearing completion and work can be seen in progress on the first passenger terminal.

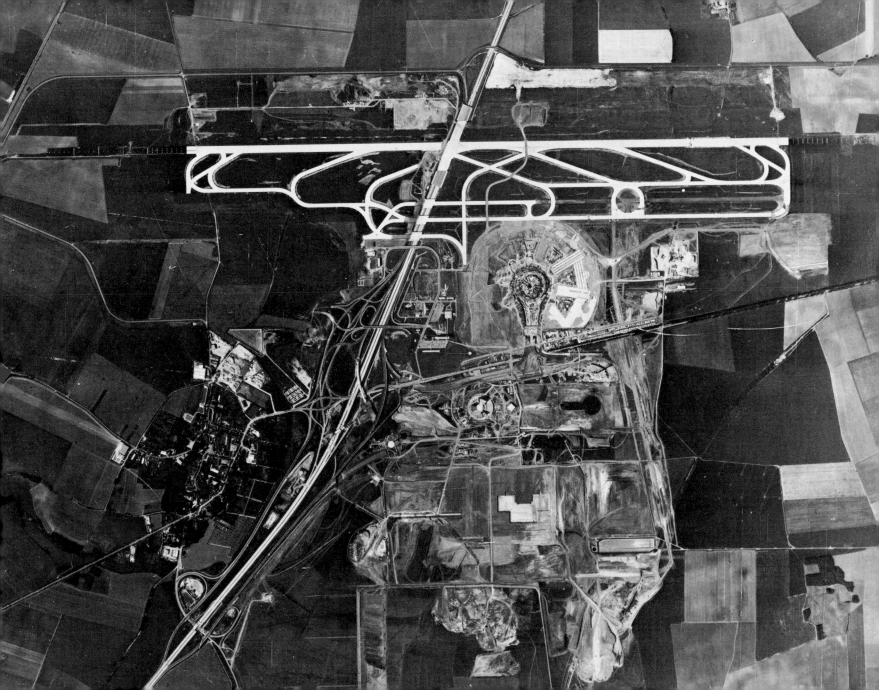

airport will be capable of handling 500,000 aircraft movements a year, with up to 150 an hour, thirty million passengers and two million tons of freight. An outstanding visual feature of the airport will be its 57·4 m (188 ft) high water tower, in appearance rather like a mushroom with a very tall slender stalk. Apart from being linked to Paris by motorways, it is possible that the new French high-speed tracked air-cushion aérotrain may operate services between Roissy-en-France and the city.

Long before the more recent boom in air traffic, the Schiphol Airport Authority had foreseen the need for very large-scale development of Amsterdam's airport and a plan had been made for extension of the airport to 1,350 hectares (3,330 acres) with a central terminal area and a tangential runway system having six runways, the longest measuring 3,300 m (10,827 ft).

Some of these runways have been constructed but the plan has been changed. There are four main runways: the main, Category II, instrument runway 01L–19R of 3,300 m (10,827 ft), 01R–19L of 3,400 m (11,155 ft), 06–24 of 3,250 m (10,663 ft) and 09–27 of 3,453 m (11,330 ft). There are plans for a possible fifth main runway, 01LL–19RR, which would increase airport capacity and reduce community noise. In addition, the older runways 05–23 and 14–32 are still in existence and measure 2,020 m

(6,626 ft) and 1,800 m (5,905 ft) respectively.

Runway 01L–19R has edge and centreline lights throughout its length, green threshold lights, and white barrette touchdown zone lighting extending for 900 m (2,950 ft) from the threshold. The approach lights consist of barrettes forming a white centreline over a distance of 900 m (2,950 ft) with white crossbars at 300 m (985 ft) and 150 m (492 ft) before the threshold. In addition there is a row of red barrettes on each side of the centreline for the final 270 m (885 ft) of the approach.

Runways 01R, 06 and 27 have line and bar approach lights with red barrettes for 268 m (880 ft) before the thresholds, and there is white touchdown zone lighting on the first 914 m (3,000 ft) of runways 01R, 19L and 27.

The Schiphol terminal building comprises a main block with three traffic piers, the centre one of which has a Y-branch at its outer end. There were loading positions, with aero-bridges for 25 aircraft, but since the terminal was opened in April 1967 additional extension has taken place and further phases of the plan call for 45 aircraft positions and the ability to handle twelve million passengers a year. Another traffic pier is due for completion in 1974, a second terminal building may be required by 1980 and a second complete terminal area by 1988. Traffic forecasts have indicated the possibility of Amsterdam

Schiphol Airport, Amsterdam. This view, looking southeast, ▶ shows runway 01L–19R in the foreground with 09–27, left centre. Beyond these are the terminal area and the other main runways.

having to handle 390,000 aircraft movements, 63 million passengers and six million tons of cargo annually by the year 2000.

In Scandinavia there has also been much airport development in recent years. Copenhagen/Kastrup had a completely new terminal opened in 1960 and nine years later a separate domestic terminal was opened. Kastrup has staggered parallel southwest–northeast runways of 3,300 m (10,827 ft) and 3,600 m (11,811 ft) and a northwest–southeast runway of 3,060 m (10,039 ft). There is also a shorter east–west runway.

Kastrup is situated right on the shores of Öresund and part of the airport is on reclaimed land. This makes the extension of runways almost impossible because of conflict with the shipping lanes. The airport handled more than 150,000 aircraft movements and about 6½ million passengers in 1970, and as traffic increases a new airport will almost certainly be necessary. Consideration has been given to siting an airport on the island of Saltholm in Öresund so that it could serve both Denmark and southern Sweden.

In Norway, Fornebu Airport has been extended to handle jet aircraft in spite of the closeness of the airport to the city of Oslo and the problems of difficult terrain. In addition airports have been constructed throughout the length of the country so that

landplanes have now replaced the flying-boats and seaplanes formerly used. Probably one of the greatest feats of airport building took place near Bergen when Flesland Airport was built. The only available area for an airport had numerous rocky hills and valleys and NATO said it was impossible to build an aerodrome in the area. But the Norwegians demolished the hills and used the stone and earth to fill the valleys and now have a modern airport with a runway 2,450 m (8,038 ft) long from which North Atlantic services are operated.

Stockholm's old Bromma Airport is still in use for domestic services but a new airport, Arlanda, is the international airport and provides a take-off run of 3,300 m (10,827 ft). In Helsinki, also, a new airport has been constructed. This has a recently opened terminal and its longest runway measures 3,200 m (10,500 ft).

Germany handles very heavy air traffic and it is therefore natural that a lot of airport development has taken place there. The old Frankfurt/Rhein Main Airport still serves the city but it is a very changed place to that from which pre-war Zeppelins flew to America. There are parallel concrete runways, 07L–25R being 3,900 m (12,795 ft) long and 07R–25L having a length of 3,750 m (12,303 ft). All approaches except to 07R have centreline and bar approach lights and those leading to the longest

Zürich International Airport. The terminal and curved apron is in the centre
and the Swissair maintenance base is beyond.

runway have sequenced flashers on the centreline. A north–south runway is to be provided and it is planned that the existing runways will be lengthened. Somewhere around ten million passengers a year are using Frankfurt Airport and a large new terminal has been constructed to handle this traffic. There are parking stands for more than seventy aircraft.

Many other German airports are being rebuilt with new terminals, and Hamburg and Munich are to have completely new airports because it is impossible to expand the existing airports sufficiently to cope with future traffic.

The main Swiss airports are still Geneva and Zürich. The present Geneva Airport is the original Cointrin, greatly enlarged. It now has a paved runway of 3,900 m (12,795 ft), a large terminal opened in 1968, and, on the parking apron, three circular satellite buildings which are connected to the main terminal by tunnels which contain moving walkways.

Zürich's Dübendorf Airport was inadequate for post-war development, so in 1945 it was decided to build a new airport at Kloten and only three years later the first runway was in operation. When the new Zürich terminal was opened it was one of the most modern anywhere, but it soon proved too small and continuous expansion of terminal facilities and runways has taken place. There are three runways, the main instrument runway, 16–34, being 3,700 m (12,139 ft) long and having line and bar approach lights to its northern end. The airport elevation is 431 m (1,414 ft). In 1970 Geneva Airport handled 113,000 aircraft movements and $2\frac{3}{4}$ million passengers, and the figures for Zürich were 130,000 movements and $4\frac{1}{2}$ million passengers.

For many years after the war Ciampino was Rome's airport, but its potential was limited and a new airport was constructed close to the mouth of the Tiber. Officially named Leonardo da Vinci Airport but more generally known as Fiumicino, the new airport has a large terminal building, is the main base of Alitalia, and has two paved runways – the longest, 16–34, being 3,901 m (12,800 ft).

This brief survey of European airports must suffice for it is only possible here to mention a few and give a picture of their main features. All the major cities have their airports and many new ones will be constructed during the next ten to twenty years. But it is not only the main industrial and commercial centres which have airports. In recent years there has been an enormous growth of airborne holiday traffic, and airports formerly serving small communities have had to be expanded to handle heavy concentrated loads of holidaymakers. For example, Palma de Mallorca's Son San Juan Airport handled more than 67,000 aircraft movements and nearly five million passengers in 1970 and this type of traffic is growing rapidly.

In addition to all the main and secondary airports, Europe is gradually developing STOLports to bring air transport to the more isolated communities, and high in the French Alps there are altiports to cater for winter sports traffic. These specialised landing grounds are described in a later chapter.

8

Middle East, Africa and Asia

The airports of this vast region have been grouped here because there are no firmly defined boundaries to these areas. For example, Beirut and Cairo are the two most important airports in the Middle East but the former is in Asia and the latter in Africa.

Beirut and Cairo sit astride the great trunk air routes linking Europe with Africa, India, the Far East and Australasia, and during the development of these trunk routes Cairo was always an important junction. Beirut has established its importance on the air routes in the post-war years and in this latter period an important regional network of air services has been developed throughout the Middle East.

Because of the vast deserts stretching right across North Africa and Arabia and beyond into Central Asia, many of the towns and cities are physically as separated as if they were islands in an enormous ocean – for this reason the aeroplane has become the prime form of transport.

Beirut International Airport is in a superb situation between the Mediterranean and the coastal mountain range and is an appropriate gateway to the eastern Mediterranean and Asia. It has a large terminal standing at the head of a long straight highway leading to the city, and two runways, 03–21 and 18–36, providing a maximum take-off run of 10,500 ft (3,200 m).

Cairo's airport is at an elevation of 336 ft (112 m) in the desert to the east of the city, quite near to the older Almaza Airport, and has a large terminal and two main runways with a maximum length of 10,827 ft (3,300 m) provided by runway 05–23. The approaches to the southern end of the 16–34 runway are over sandhills and have at times been subject to criticism on safety grounds, but it is understood that improved aids have now made this runway acceptable.

The large-scale development, made possible by oil royalties, of the Gulf states has led to the construction of a number of new and well-equipped airports and the complete reconstruction of others. Most have runways of 9,000 to 12,000 ft (2,743–3,657 m), and some of the terminal buildings have outstanding architectural merit. The first of these was at Dhahran in Saudi Arabia, where the structure comprises a series of columns with flattened umbrella-like tops that form a roof composed of large canopies – this system being known as a hyperbolic paraboloid. More recent examples of this type are those at Dubai where the terminal was opened in May 1971, in modified form at Abu Dhabi, opened in 1970, and at the new Newark terminals in New Jersey.

Bahrein's airport occupies the same site as its first primitive airport forty years ago but is now a modern airport with a new terminal and a 12,000 ft (3,657 m) runway. The new Kuwait Airport has an 11,152 ft (3,352 m) runway and that at Doha has been

The attractive terminal building at Dubai International Airport.
The aircraft is a Boeing 707 of Saudi Arabian Airlines.

A Fokker F.28 Fellowship on the packed-sand runway at Illizi in Algeria.

extended to 15,000 ft (4,572 m), making it one of the longest in the world.

Saudi Arabia, in addition to Dhahran, has major airports at Jeddah, Medina and Riyadh. Jeddah has to handle very large numbers of Muslim Hadj pilgrims to Mecca, and much of the present airport terminal building is devoted to pilgrim accommoda-tion. The airport itself is virtually in the city and joins the built-up area on two of its boundaries, but a new airport, north of the city, is planned. There are plans for improving Riyadh Airport and many of the other Saudi airports are to be modernised.

Baghdad, Damascus, Amman, Jerusalem, Lod and other airports all play a part in Middle East air transport, as does the 3,949 ft (1,203 m) high Mehrabad Airport at Teheran in Iran which is due to be replaced in 1977 by one of four times the capacity.

Africa is a large continent with a population in excess of 300 million, but its air traffic represents only a small part of the world total. The continent's population concentrations are in the northwest close to the Mediterranean, along the Nile valley, in West Africa, and then more evenly distributed in the southern half of the continent. A very large area in the north is desert and sparsely populated. Much of the eastern and southern areas are at high elevations.

Most of the North African countries have domestic route networks using airports of widely varying standard and at least one major airport each which serves international and regional traffic. Several of the major airports require improved runways and few have adequate terminals. On the domestic routes aircraft frequently land on rough desert runways, some of which are more than generously covered by loose stones.

In West Africa, too, there is wide variation in airport standards, although the main airports such as Dakar (Sénégal), Abidjan (Ivory Coast), Roberts-field (Liberia), Accra (Ghana) and Lagos (Nigeria) all handle large jet aircraft, while small twin-jets

operate some domestic services in Nigeria.

The airports at Accra, Abidjan, Dakar and Robertsfield are all only between 30 and 205 ft (9 and 63 m) above sea level and have runways of around 9,000 ft (2,743 m) in length, but Lagos is something of a problem airport because of high temperatures combined with a runway of only 7,600 ft (2,317 m). In the northern desert area of Nigeria, Kano Airport is at an elevation of 1,563 ft (476 m) and provides a runway length of 8,610 ft (2,624 m).

Along the Nile the Arab Republic in Egypt and the Sudan maintain airports at most of the places used by the pioneer trunk services, but apart from Cairo the only airport used by international carriers is Khartoum. Further south, on the shores of Lake Victoria, is Uganda's important Entebbe Airport with a 9,875 ft (3,010 m) runway at an elevation of 3,789 ft (1,155 m).

For many years Nairobi, at a height of well over 5,000 ft (1,525 m), had two airports – the joint civil/military aerodrome of Eastleigh for international long-haul services and Wilson Airport for local and regional services. But in March 1958 a new airport was opened at Embakasi, close to the game park. The airport now has a 13,507 ft (4,117 m) runway and is the city's main air terminal although the much smaller Wilson Airport is still in operation.

Tanzania's main airports are at Dar-es-Salaam

and Arusha, the latter being a new international airport opened in December 1971 and named Kilimanjaro after Africa's highest mountain which is closeby.

Zaire, formerly the Belgian Congo, has a large number of airports, many with short unpaved runways, but Kinshasa, the capital, has a paved runway, 07–25, of 15,420 ft (4,700 m) at an elevation of 1,004 ft (306 m).

Rhodesia, Malawi, Zambia and the Republic of South Africa all have their airport systems which cater for long-distance, regional and local services. The most important airport in the Republic of South Africa is Jan Smuts, about 15 miles (24 km) from Johannesburg. This is at an elevation of 5,559 ft (1,695 m) and its 03–21 runway is 14,500 ft (4,420 m) long. Work is in hand to enable the airport to handle twenty million passengers a year.

Asia, in general, has a much more highly developed air transport system than Africa. India, Pakistan, the Philippines, Indonesia and Japan have large domestic route networks as well as regional and international long-distance services, and Japan has been recording one of the highest growth rates achieved by air transport.

In the pioneering days of airline operation, Karachi was the gateway to India and although Karachi is now in Pakistan its airport is of great importance and serves as the main base of Pakistan International Airlines. The terminal buildings are of pre-war origin but with modifications, and a completely new terminal is planned. The single main runway, 07L–25R, is 10,500 ft (3,200 m) long. Pakistan has other important airports at Lahore, Rawalpindi, Peshawar, Quetta and elsewhere, but its most interesting airports are those in the far north and to the west in Baluchistan.

The world's greatest mountain ranges stretch across the north of Pakistan and these make surface transport difficult and, at times, dangerous. As a result, since its inception Pakistan has had to supply Gilgit and Skardu, in Kashmir, by air. In the days of the DC-3 this involved flying through the Indus valley with towering mountains on either side, but today the Fokker Friendships fly at greater heights although they must still let down among the mountains to land at Gilgit, 4,770 ft (1,454 m) above sea level, and Skardu at an elevation of 7,600 ft (2,316 m). Their runway lengths are respectively 5,400 ft (1,645 m) and 5,100 ft (1,554 m). The Skardu runway is unpaved and aircraft taking-off and landing trail behind them great plumes of dust. In a similar situation is Chitral in the northwest of Pakistan. This airport has to be approached through a valley, it is 4,900 ft (1,493 m) above sea level and its unpaved runway, with a liberal covering of

stones, is 6,000 ft (1,829 m) long. The Baluchistan aerodromes include a sunbaked mud area serving Pasni and the old Imperial Airways stony landing ground at Gwadar close to the great eroded 'Cathedral Rock'.

India has four main international airports, Bombay, Delhi, Calcutta and Madras, and a large number of airports from Trivandrum in the far south to Kashmir in the north. Bombay's Santacruz Airport, to the north of the city, is the main base of Air-India and serves many foreign airlines. It has two runways, the longest being the 11,005 ft (3,354 m) 09–27. This runway was originally much shorter and had to be lengthened to accommodate jet aircraft – a formidable task because of a range of hills close to its eastern threshold, which it was feared consisted of rock. But to everyone's delight they were found to be of earth and their tops were removed.

Palam replaced Safdarjung (formerly Willingdon Airport) as Delhi's main airport, and this provides a maximum take-off run of 12,500 ft (3,810 m). Palam is the main base of Indian Airlines and this operator carries well over two million passengers a year on its Indian domestic and regional services with a fleet which includes Boeing 737 and Caravelle twin-jet aircraft.

The Calcutta Airport has been developed on the site of the pre-war Dum Dum and its runways have a maximum length of 10,500 ft (3,200 m). The Madras Airport is also one that has been expanded on its original site, at St Thomas' Mount.

In addition to these main airports, a number of others can handle jet aircraft and these include Agra, close to the Taj Mahal, Bangalore, Hyderabad, Lucknow and Nagpur which is the junction point for the Indian night air mail services which serve the four main cities.

Burma has numerous airports serving domestic flights as well as Mingaladon at Rangoon which is another example of a present day airport still operating on its pre-war site.

An airport of great importance in the Far East air transport system is Bangkok's Don Muang – yet one more airport developed on a pre-war site. Bangkok is a junction for services to Hongkong and Tokyo and those continuing to Singapore and Australia. Don Muang has parallel runways, 03–21, and the longest measures 10,525 ft (3,208 m). In recent times the rather picturesque terminal gave way to a modern air-conditioned building, but now the decision has been taken to construct an entirely new international airport 25 km (15 miles) southeast of the city and the first phase of a 25-year development programme should be completed by 1977. Meanwhile the existing airport is to be expanded to cope with the increasing traffic.

◀ Gilgit Airport in Pakistani Kashmir. The Gilgit River is in the foreground and some of the world's most spectacular mountains start to rise immediately beyond the airport.

Hongkong's Kai Tak Airport at dusk, with the runway extending into Kowloon Bay. Some of the approach lights can be seen leading across the heavily built-up Kowloon City area in the foreground.

In Malaysia, Kuala Lumpur has a modern airport with a large terminal and an 11,400 ft (3,475 m) runway which was essential before regular jet operations could begin.

Ever since the early 1930s Singapore Airport has been of great importance and, as recorded elsewhere in this book, the city had a fine airport before the war. But this proved too small for modern aircraft and could not be extended. Work on the new

Singapore/Paya Lebar Airport began in 1952 and it was opened in 1955, with a single runway and a temporary terminal. There is now a large terminal building handling well over a million passengers a year and there are several large hangars. The runway, 02–20, is 11,000 ft (3,352 m) long and equipped with modified Calvert line and bar approach lighting at each end.

Space does not permit descriptions of all the large

number of Asian airports, including those in the Philippines and Indonesia, but because of their importance the Hongkong and Tokyo airports must be described at some length.

The governing factor in airport design at Hongkong has always been topography. The area is extremely mountainous and the original Kai Tak Airport was constructed on a small flat shoreside area opposite Hongkong Island. In order to ac-commodate larger and faster aircraft the tops of some of the mountains were removed, but eventually it became necessary to rebuild the airport completely and this was achieved by constructing a single runway and parallel taxiway out into Kowloon Bay, and a new terminal on the site of the old airport. The runway, 13–31, is 8,350 ft (2,545 m) long but further reclamation is in hand to extend it to a total length of 11,130 ft (3,392 m), with the extension due to

This view of a Qantas Boeing 707 well illustrates the landward approach to Hongkong Airport.

come into operation in the summer of 1973. Approach lighting is installed at each end of the runway and Hongkong is probably unique in having the approach lights, to its landward end, form a curving instead of a straight lead-in line. This unusual layout is necessary because of the proximity of the mountains, and the final approach from this end has to be made at low altitude over a heavily built-up area.

Japan has a very high volume of air traffic, particularly over such routes as Tokyo–Osaka, Tokyo–Sapporo and Tokyo–Fukuoka, and the present Tokyo International Airport (Haneda) handles well over ten million passengers a year. Haneda, on the shores of Tokyo Bay, is a pre-war airport and now has paved runways, the longest, 15L–33R, being 10,335 ft (3,150 m). It also has the rare distinction of having a monorail connection to the city.

The rapid growth of international and domestic traffic made it essential to find a site for an additional and much bigger Tokyo airport. A site was found at Narita *66 km (41 miles)* northeast of Tokyo and, in spite of riots by local farmers, students and other opponents of the airport, work progressed rapidly and the first phase of the airport was opened in 1972.

The new Tokyo International Airport has an area of 1,065 hectares (about 2,556 acres) and will eventually have two parallel runways, one of 4,000 m (13,123 ft) and the other 2,500 m (8,200 ft) with 2,500 m separation. Linking the two will be a 3,200 m (10,500 ft) crosswind runway. Passenger and cargo terminals are between the first runway and the central access road. The second and third runways, with additional taxiways, will be built under Phase 2 but before this stage is implemented the new airport will be capable of handling 5·4 million passengers and 410,000 tons of cargo annually, and its passenger terminal with four satellites will provide 32 gate-positions with ability to accommodate twenty DC-8s or similar aircraft and up to twelve Boeing 747s.

Although the new airport will be three times the size of Haneda, the older airport is to be provided with two additional runways and is to be capable of handling 50 million passengers a year by 1985.

Little is known about Chinese airports except that Peking, Canton and Shanghai can handle jet aircraft in the Boeing 707 and Ilyushin Il-62 category. Peking has a large, but old fashioned, terminal building and, in general, the traffic volume appears to be small. The main airports are known to have ILS installations.

9

Australasia

Australia is a continent of vast empty spaces of desert and bush country and its sparse population either congregates in the littoral cities or occupies small townships or lonely homesteads across the country.

The country possesses one of the world's finest air transport systems and, in spite of its small population, its two major domestic airlines – TAA - Trans-Australia Airlines and Ansett – carry a total of about six million passengers a year. There are the main international airports, others serving the smaller cities, and a large number of simple airports and landing grounds serving the outback communities. In addition many of the sheep stations have their own runways which will take quite large aircraft.

Darwin in the Northern Territory was the arrival point of the first flight from Europe to Australia, at the end of 1919, and Darwin's present 11,000 ft (3,352 m) runway is used by some international services, but the major Australian airports are those serving Brisbane, Sydney, Melbourne, Adelaide and Perth.

Brisbane has had two airports, Archerfield and Eagle Farm, and it is the latter which is used today and provides a longest run of 7,760 ft (2,347 m). It was at Eagle Farm that Kingsford Smith's Fokker *Southern Cross* landed in June 1928 after making the first flight across the Pacific and the aircraft is now preserved in its own memorial hall at the airport. Brisbane's Archerfield Airport was the original terminal of the England–Australia service.

Since the war Sydney has been the most important Australian air traffic centre. The present airport, now known as Kingsford Smith but formerly as

Mascot, has been developed on the site used since 1920 when it was a 160 acre (64 hectare) cow pasture.

Sydney's airport is only a few miles south of the city and on the shores of Botany Bay. There are two runways, 07–25 of 8,290 ft (2,527 m) and 16–34 of 9,100 ft (2,773 m). When jet aircraft were introduced 07–25 was the main runway although the Boeing 727s could operate from 16–34 which had a length of 5,700 ft (1,737 m). Large-scale reclamation and the sinking of the General Holmes Drive motorway to pass under the runway enabled extension to 9,100 ft, and this runway is being extended even further into Botany Bay to give a total length of 13,000 ft (3,962 m).

For many years the terminal area at Sydney was in the northeast angle of the runways. TAA and Ansett had their own, quite attractive, terminals but the international terminal was not of the standard suitable for such an important airport. In May 1970 a new international terminal was opened near the western boundary of the airport, a three-storey building 680 ft (207 m) long and 235 ft (72 m) deep. Projecting from it onto the apron is a Y-shaped pier which is in effect an elevated two-deck concourse, some 1,200 ft (365 m) long, which provides waiting rooms and aero-bridges at seven of the loading positions – two gates being for Boeing 747s.

In mid-1972 a study was commissioned to examine further possible development of Sydney Airport and plans for a second airport.

Australia's latest airport is Melbourne's Tulla-marine, officially opened on 1 July 1970 as the replacement for Essendon which had long served the city but was inadequate for the bigger jet aircraft. Tullamarine, which is about 12½ miles (20 km) northwest of Melbourne, occupies an area of about 5,300 acres (2,120 hectares) and has two runways. The main runway, aligned approximately north–south, is 8,500 ft (2,590 m) long and will be extended to 12,000 ft (3,657 m). The secondary runway, approximately east–west, is 7,500 ft (2,286 m) long and can be extended at its western end. The terminal area is to the east of the main runway and provision has been made for a similar runway layout south of it to provide two pairs of parallel runways with a minimum lateral separation of about 6,000 ft (1,830 m).

The Tullamarine terminal is in the form of a flattened U with a central international block 320 ft (97 m) long, flanked by 200 ft (60 m) long domestic wings. Three traffic piers project onto the apron and some loading positions are equipped with aero-bridges. Initially eight international and twenty domestic loading-positions were provided plus four stand-by positions, but the master plan allows for

The terminal building, loading aprons, carparks, and approach roads
at the new Tullamarine Airport, Melbourne.

sixteen international and sixty domestic boarding-gates. The airport has a 150 ft (45 m) high control tower.

Adelaide has a pleasant airport with two runways and Perth provides a maximum take-off run of 10,300 ft (3,140 m).

Also coming under Australian administration are the airports in the New Guinea/Papua area. Those at Port Moresby, Lae and some other points are quite orthodox, but many used by scheduled services are nothing short of spectacular. Some are situated at high elevations on mountainsides, have steep gradients demanding uphill landings and downhill take-offs, and have deep ravines running alongside.

Many of these aerodromes, with grass or earth surfaces, can only be used by light transport aircraft, but DC-3s have for years been regular users of the grass aerodrome at Wau. This is several hundred feet higher at one end than at the other and, apart from landing uphill, aircraft have to be parked sideways to ensure that they do not run away. A damaged Bristol Freighter which did run away is used as living accommodation by coffee plantation workers. One spectacular aerodrome is that at Omkali (Omkolai) where the 1,700 ft (518 m) strip at an elevation of 5,500 ft (1,675 m) has a gradient of 13 per cent and is right on the edge of a mountain with a 1,200 ft (365 m) almost sheer drop to a river running through a vee-shaped valley. In many places these mountainside aerodromes offer the only means of communication with the outside world – for the alternatives are to make the journey by air in minutes or at the most a few hours, or to spend days or weeks walking across the mountains and through the jungles.

The mountainous terrain of New Zealand's North and South Islands has always made the provision of adequate airports difficult, and at the present time there are only four airports which handle commercial jet aircraft. Douglas DC-8s of Air New Zealand operate from Auckland, Christchurch and Wellington and the New Zealand National Airways

Against a striking background of New Zealand's Southern Alps, a Fox Moth lands at one of the pre-war grass aerodromes used by the mail services.

Corporation's Boeing 737s also serve Dunedin.

Christchurch has an 8,014 ft (2,442 m) runway and Auckland one of 8,500 ft (2,590 m) but the Wellington runway – the construction of which was a major engineering feat – starts at the edge of Cook Strait and ends at the shore of Evans Bay and is only 5,350 ft (1,630 m) long.

Australasia [85]

◀ Omkali, or Omkolai, landing ground in the New Guinea Highlands. With mountains at each end and a sheer drop on one side, this runway is used by regular scheduled air services.

10

Canada and the North Atlantic

Canada has long been a country dependent on air transport for communication with its remoter areas. In the early days most of its air operations were from railheads into the north, and many of the aircraft were seaplanes alighting on rivers and lakes in summer and fitted with skis for winter operation. By 1938 a system of airports had been established right across the country and a transcontinental air mail service was in operation.

Today the main Canadian cities have modern airports capable of handling the largest jet aircraft, and there are large numbers of smaller airports for regional services. But seaplanes are still widely used for the transport of passengers and cargo in some areas.

Montreal's Dorval Airport has played a major part in the history of Canadian air transport and it was an extremely important war-time aerodrome, serving as the western base for the transatlantic ferry organisation. Although the airport has a large modern terminal with a satellite for some international and domestic operations and its 06L–24R runway provides a length of 11,000 ft (3,352 m), it has been decided that the airport cannot be expanded sufficiently to meet the long-term needs of the area.

The Canadian Government took the bold step of expropriating 90,000 acres (about 35,000 hectares) of land in the Ste-Scholastique area northwest of Montreal for development of a new airport. Within this area the airport's operational zone will occupy about 20,000 acres (8,000 hectares) while 70,000 acres (28,000 hectares) will come within the noise zone. By acquiring such a large area the Government will be able to protect the future growth of the

Calgary Airport in Alberta. The Rocky Mountains can be seen in the background.

airport and ensure that it fits into the environment without causing disturbance.

In the first phase, due for completion in 1974, there will be two runways, 11L–29R and 06RC–24LC, each of about 3,600 m (11,811 ft), a passenger terminal, cargo and aircraft maintenance buildings and other essential facilities. In the final plan there is provision for the lengthening of runway 06RC–24LC, construction of three more 06–24 runways and a second 11–29. Considerable space is being reserved for additional passenger and cargo terminals, for a STOLport, and for some form of mass transport system linking the airport with the city. In Phase 1 the airport will occupy 3,500 acres (1,415 hectares).

Apart from Dorval, a number of Canadian airports have been closely linked with the development of North Atlantic air routes. Although it is now a

An Air Canada Douglas DC-8 on the loading apron in front of Toronto Airport's terminal building.

regular daily occurrence for large-capacity jet airliners to fly from Europe nonstop to New York and, over a much greater distance, to the US West Coast, for many years the Atlantic was a major obstacle to aircraft.

The shortest direct crossing of the ocean is between the Republic of Ireland and Newfoundland, although

shorter ocean sectors can be achieved by flying from Europe via Iceland and Greenland to Labrador, and, before transatlantic air services began, surveys were made of both routes as well as one via the Azores and Bermuda.

The earliest transatlantic air services, operated by Britain and the USA, were worked by flying-boats, but during the war large numbers of landplanes crossed the ocean, and when commercial services began after the war they too were operated by landplanes.

Two airports, one each side of the ocean, played an essential part in the war-time operations. These were Prestwick in southwest Scotland and Gander in Newfoundland. Also of great importance was Goose Bay in Labrador. Keflavik in Iceland and airports on the west coast of Greenland also played a prominent rôle.

When civil operations by landplanes began, Shannon Airport in the south of Ireland became the main European gateway airport. Gander was first choice of airports on the western side of the ocean although others were used, mainly for bad weather diversions.

One of the problems of operating North Atlantic services is the prevailing westerly wind which can be very strong, thus reducing the range of aircraft on westbound flights. Boeing Stratocruisers and some other types could frequently fly nonstop from New York to London and the nearer European airports; but it was not until the appearance of the Bristol Britannia, Douglas DC-7C and Lockheed L.1649 in 1956–57 that regular nonstop operation could be achieved in both directions. Indeed, on introducing its Britannias at the end of 1957, El Al produced a

A recent photograph of Prestwick Airport, Ayrshire. The main runway, 13–31, runs diagonally across the picture and part of runway 03–21 can be seen on the right.

clever advertisement proclaiming 'No Goose, No Gander'. When the first jets appeared on the Atlantic in 1958, they were still short of range and refuelling stops were again necessary, but soon longer-range versions were introduced and most of the Atlantic airports lost their former importance.

Goose and Gander and some of the other Canadian airports continue to serve domestic and non-scheduled services but their major rôle in history has now ended. Prestwick (12,000 transport aircraft movements and 500,000 passengers in 1970–71) serves as the long-haul international airport for Scotland and has a 9,800 ft (2,987 m) runway. Shannon is now important in its own right as the gateway to Ireland – Dublin Airport never having been opened to non-Irish Atlantic airlines. One of Shannon's attractions has long been the fact that it is a customs-free airport.

Keflavik still maintains a place on the Atlantic air routes because the Reykjavik Airport cannot handle large aircraft. In Greenland, Søndrestrømfjord, earlier known as Bluie West Eight, was a refuelling point when Scandinavian Airlines System (SAS) opened its so-called Polar route to North America but this airport has now lost much of its importance.

The Azores now have their own domestic air services and have ceased to play a major Atlantic rôle, while Bermuda Airport is used by heavy tourist traffic to the islands and is a refuelling stop for aircraft flying further into the Caribbean area and, in some cases, on to the Pacific.

Bermuda Airport can be seen occupying most of St David's Island and with the short runway projecting into Castle Harbour.

11

Latin America

Central and South America have a long air transport history stretching back more than fifty years. In Brazil and Colombia many of the early air services were worked by flying-boats and seaplanes, and services up the Amazon were operated by flying-boats until recent years. Airports were established along the east coast, in Chile, and into the far south of the Argentine for the pioneer air mail services operated by France in association with various South American companies.

The major cities of South America have their international airports and, serving the various domestic and regional route systems, there are large numbers of airports, including many which simply comprise a short unpaved runway.

Brazil claims one of the airports closest to the city it serves. This is Santos Dumont Airport at Rio de Janeiro which is very small and right alongside the built-up area; it was the city's main airport but now only handles local services, the main airport being Galeao which has a 10,827 ft (3,300 m) runway. Bolivia can claim what is almost certainly the highest major airport in the world, if not the highest of any kind. It is La Paz in the Andes, 13,355 ft (4,070 m) above sea level, and its 09–27 runway is 13,123 ft (4,000 m) long. There are runway and threshold lights but no approach lights.

An example of an undeveloped South American airport is Itabuna in Brazil. Although at low elevation, this airport has a sandy swampy surface with an available take-off distance of only 3,937 ft (1,200 m) and endures temperatures of around 40 degrees C (104 degrees F). In spite of the poor surface, short length and high temperatures, the twin-jet Fokker

A Hawker Siddeley 748 taking-off from an unpaved runway in Chile, with the Andes forming the background.

(2,105 m) 18–36 runway at La Rioja in the Argentine at an elevation of 1,414 ft (430 m) in a temperature of 22 degrees C (71·6 degrees F).

Although these are just two examples of primitive South American airports, there are many more. They provide an important service in making air transport possible in remote areas; but it must not be assumed that all South American airports come into this category. Ezeiza, the main Buenos Aires airport, has a 10,825 ft (3,299 m) runway with runway, threshold and approach lighting; Pudahuel at Santiago in Chile has a 10,499 ft (3,200 m) paved runway with full lighting; and Caracas in Venezuela has Maiquetia Airport with a 9,843 ft (3,000 m) runway. In Colombia, Bogota's Eldorado Airport is at an elevation of 8,355 ft (2,546 m) and has a 12,467 ft (3,800 m) runway, but no approach lighting.

Another high altitude airport is Mexico City's Central Airport which is at 7,347 ft (2,240 m) and has a 10,824 ft (3,299 m) main runway. Acapulco International Airport, on Mexico's Pacific coast, has a runway of identical length to that at Mexico City and from it aircraft can operate with sufficient fuel to fly the 3,609 nautical-mile (6,688 km) stage to Tahiti. But, like the other Latin-American countries, Mexico has its share of smaller airports with unpaved runways, some as short as 3,000 ft (914 m).

F.28 Fellowship has landed there. The same aircraft has also operated from the unpaved stony 6,906 ft

12

Island Airports

Islands have played an important part in the development of air transport because they acted as stepping stones for aircraft which had insufficient range to make nonstop ocean crossings. In return aircraft have made great contributions to the economies of island communities by providing them with rapid and reliable communication.

The Azores, Bermuda, Iceland, Greenland and Newfoundland have contributed to the air conquest of the North Atlantic as mentioned in Chapter 10, but the island airport's greatest contribution has been in the Pacific where distances are great.

Honolulu International is a major airport handling heavy traffic to and from the United States mainland, and serves as a refuelling point for aircraft flying between North America and the Far East and on the routes to Australia and New Zea-

land. Further south are two important island airports, Nadi (pronounced Nandi) in Fiji and Papeete in Tahiti. Fiji and Honolulu split the Sydney–San Francisco route into three quite convenient stages of 1,728, 2,792 and 2,105 nautical miles (3,200, 5,275 and 3,900 km). Papeete is a convenient junction point for services between Mexico and Fiji and for trans-Pacific services from South America via the airport on Easter Island.

Honolulu International Airport has a large terminal building and a separate domestic terminal and its longest runway measures 12,380 ft (3,773 m). Fiji's Nadi has two runways – the longest being 10,500 ft (3,200 m) – but geographical and meteorological conditions dictated that it should be sited on the opposite end of the main island Viti Levu to Suva, Fiji's capital, and local air services connect

The runway at Savu Savu on Vanua Levu, Fiji.

Nadi with Suva's modest Nausori Airport.

Until comparatively recently Tahiti had to be served by flying-boat but now an airport (with the strange name Faaa) has been constructed alongside the lagoon near Papeete and this has a single runway, 04–22, of 11,204 ft (3,215 m).

There are numerous other Pacific islands which possess airports, such as Canton Island, Guam, Midway, and Wake Island, but many have now lost their importance because of increased aircraft range. However, Pago Pago (pronounced Pango Pango) in Samoa is coming into prominence, largely because of the upsurge in Pacific area tourist travel.

In the pioneer days of long-distance air services the Indonesian islands (formerly the Netherlands East Indies) provided important stopping places on the air route between Europe and Australia, but long-range aircraft now overfly these islands, except to serve Djakarta, and the country has its own airline system.

Three Mediterranean islands have also been important refuelling points on long-distance trunk routes. Crete was used by the Imperial Airways flying-boats on the Africa and India route and in more recent times Malta and Cyprus performed this function for landplanes. Now these islands have quite heavy traffic but this is destined mainly for the islands themselves while the long-distance air-

The terminal building at Honolulu International Airport. On the apron are two United Air Lines' Douglas DC-8s and two Pan American Boeing 707s. ▶

craft trace their white contrails high overhead.

In the Indian Ocean, Mauritius is a port of call on the services of Qantas and South African Airways which link Johannesburg with Australia, but the runway in the Cocos Islands, which was built with such difficulty to serve the route, is no longer used – again because of the increased range of present aircraft.

Faaa Airport near Papeete, Tahiti. The runway is close beside the lagoon which for many years served as a flying-boat base.

13

The Soviet Union

In the USSR transport aircraft operate out of a wide range of aerodromes, from simple earth strips to the fully-equipped modern international airport, but little is known about most of these aerodromes and airports and only very few are open for non-Soviet aircraft.

It is known that within the Soviet Union some 3,500 cities, towns and settlements are served by regular air services and that, in addition, ambulance and agricultural aircraft work from a large number of landing strips throughout the country. Many aerodromes are situated at high altitude in mountainous areas and for long periods others are covered with snow and ice.

During the five years 1966–70 there were plans for building 35–40 airports of what are called all-Union significance and at least 200 smaller airports were

to have been built for local air services.

The best-known Soviet airports are those which serve the Moscow area. The earliest was the Moscow Central (Frunze) Airport which was small and has now been closely built around, although it is still used for flying, but not for the operation of scheduled services. Another early Moscow airport was Vnukovo which for many years had only what might be called a classical Croydon-like terminal building.

In more recent years Moscow has acquired two new airports and Vnukovo has been much improved. The first of the new airports was Sheremetyevo which was opened in June 1961. It has two terminals, and is used by Aeroflot's international services and all the foreign airlines serving Moscow. Cargo services also use Sheremetyevo. The airport has a single 3,500 m (11,485 ft) concrete runway with approach lights at

each end, and one of the terminals has a large circular cantilever roof reminiscent of Pan American World Airways' terminal at John F. Kennedy International Airport, New York.

The latest of the Moscow airports is Domodedovo which was opened in 1964 or 1965 and handles the Soviet long-distance domestic passenger and cargo services. The modern three-storey light metal, concrete and glass terminal has two 200 m (656 ft) traffic piers and can handle 3,000 passengers an hour.

To meet the needs of the greatly expanding traffic, the old Vnukovo terminal was enlarged and improved and a second terminal built. These are now known as Vnukovo 1 and 2, originally the former handled services to the Caucasus, Crimea and Ukraine while Vnukovo 2 mainly served the operations by the twin-jet Tupolev Tu-124s, although its main use is for official occasions and the reception of foreign dignitaries.

Many other cities have been provided with new airports or new airport terminals of modern design, and many of the earlier rather picturesque terminals, resembling wedding cakes or even wooden churches,

have disappeared or will be replaced by more functional structures. Airports known to have modern terminals, mostly of simple and pleasant design, include Leningrad-Shosseiny, Kiev-Borispol, Odessa Central, Simferopol Central, Voroshilovgrad and Zaporozh'ye.

Instrument landing systems have been installed at the main airports and the Soviet Union is working hard to reduce bad weather limits and eventually achieve blind automatic landings, certainly at international and major domestic route airports. At the present time Aeroflot aircraft are limited to 1,000 m (3,280 ft) runway visual range and 100 m (328 ft) cloud base for landings at airports with ILS, but elsewhere 30 per cent is added to these figures.

Snow and ice, combined with the darkness of the northern winter, make some Soviet airline operations extremely difficult. At major airports blowers (sometimes in the form of jet aero-engines) are used to clear snow from runways, but elsewhere it is necessary to land and take-off on snow. Some aircraft are therefore fitted with brake-equipped heated skis, and pilots are paid extra for the first landing they make on ice each day.

◀ The terminal building at Domodedovo Airport, Moscow, with four Aeroflot Ilyushin Il-18s on the snow-covered apron.

East German and Soviet Ilyushin Il-14s in front of the
Vilnius Airport terminal in 1964.

14

Marine Airports

For many years marine aircraft, that is flying-boats and seaplanes, played a major part in the development of air transport. These aircraft were in service in the largest numbers between the wars and they still did important work in many parts of the world into the 1950s. A few still survive and there is even the possibility of a small-scale revival of flying-boat services.

The world's very first air services were operated by small flying-boats when on the first day of January 1914 the St Petersburg - Tampa Airboat Line began flying regularly between St Petersburg and Tampa in Florida. The Benoist flying-boats were simple craft with open cockpits, and the facilities were equally simple – a rough plank slipway on the beach to enable the aircraft to reach the water.

After the 1914–18 war there were more flying-boat services in the United States, between Florida and Cuba, Florida and the Bahamas and Seattle and Vancouver in Canada, but much greater use of marine aircraft occurred in Europe.

The reasons for flying-boats and seaplanes being used in Europe were numerous. Water in the form of lakes, rivers, the more sheltered coastal stretches off the north German coast, and the generally calm Baltic provided ready-made aerodromes whose only cost was for slipways, hangars, buoys, and small boats to service the aircraft or patrol the alighting areas. In Scandinavia marine aircraft were employed because the terrain made construction of land airports difficult and extremely costly, and in fact marine aircraft played an important part in Norwegian air transport until very recently.

The Mediterranean and the Adriatic Seas,

although both subject to sudden changes of weather, proved suitable for marine aircraft operations. Because of the overwater distances involved in flying air services between, for example, France and Algiers and Tunis, or Rome and Tripoli, it was considered safer to operate marine aircraft at a period when engine reliability was not high and forced landings frequent, although in practice marine aircraft did not always survive an open sea alighting any better than did landplanes.

During the 1920s and 1930s a considerable network of air routes was established in the European region on which seaplanes and flying-boats proved most successful. German, Finnish and Swedish airlines worked mainly in the Baltic, and Norway developed seaplane services extending far into the Arctic. France, Italy and Spain, as Mediterranean countries, made extensive use of seaplanes and flying-boats, and Britain used flying-boats to operate the trans-Mediterranean sector of its trunk routes between the United Kingdom and India and Africa, as well as between Southampton and Guernsey in the Channel Islands. Hungary operated seaplane services on the Danube. In Switzerland small flying-boats and seaplanes operated from the lakes, but not on scheduled services.

None of these early services entailed the provision of elaborate ground facilities and, because flying

A Mediterranean stepping-stone. Imperial Airways' base at Mirabella in Crete, in 1929. The motor yacht *Imperia* and Short Calcutta and Supermarine Southampton flying-boats are seen at anchor.

was limited to daylight, it was not necessary to provide any lighting aids. Imperial Airways did, however, station the motor yacht *Imperia* in Crete to serve as a radio station and a resting place for passengers on its trans-Mediterranean services. In the Baltic area seaplanes were normally moored alongside jetties so that passengers could embark and disembark, while in the Mediterranean it was more common to moor the aircraft to a buoy, passengers being ferried by motor launch. Refuelling was also done from launches and great care had to be taken to avoid them damaging the thin hulls of the flying-boats and the floats of the seaplanes.

Marine aircraft, mostly seaplanes, were much used in the early days of air transport in Canada and Alaska where lakes and rivers served as aerodromes; but in these northern areas the climate had a marked influence on operations and the most common practice was to operate the aircraft as seaplanes in summer and to fit them with skis in the winter. Seaplanes still do much important work in Canada. In general, facilities provided in North America were even more primitive than those in Europe.

In the 1930s when the transocean routes were pioneered, the big flying-boat and, to a lesser extent, the seaplane were regarded as essential for long-distance overwater flying although, strangely, the first direct flight across the North Atlantic was made by a landplane – the Vickers Vimy of Alcock and Brown – and the first flights across the Pacific and between Australia and New Zealand were both made by a landplane – the Fokker F.VII-3m *Southern Cross* flown by Charles Kingsford Smith and C. T. P. Ulm.

The greatest name in the pioneering and development of transocean air services was Pan American Airways. This company began its activities in the Caribbean area and quickly extended its operations until it had regular passenger services, with flying-boats operating the entire journey between Florida and Buenos Aires in the Argentine. At Dinner Key, Miami, Pan American used a large houseboat as its passenger terminal and passengers embarked from a small jetty, but soon the airline constructed there what was probably the finest marine airport in the world. This terminal at Dinner Key comprised a passenger terminal building with four covered walkways leading to the flying-boat loading-positions. There were three hangars with slipways into the water and there was also a moving pontoon for lifting flying-boats out of the water.

Having established these Latin American operations, Pan American set about developing regular services across the Pacific. This was a vast undertaking because no aircraft at that time had the range to make a nonstop ocean crossing. The route had therefore to be flown in stages, using Hawaii, Midway Island, Wake Island and Guam as stepping stones to reach Manila, in the Philippines, and Hongkong.

Bases had to be set up on each island and at some of them *everything* required, including drinking water, had to be taken in by sea. But in a remarkably short time the bases were completed, with accommodation for passengers and staff, embarkation jetties, and meteorological and refuelling facilities. The service between San Francisco and Manila opened for the

carriage of mail in November 1935 and passengers were carried from October 1936.

One United States marine airport which deserves mention is the unique Catalina Airport at Avalon on Santa Catalina Island off the California coast. This had a short slipway at the head of which was a turntable which was used to turn the amphibians about forty-five degrees so that they could taxi up a ramp to the parking area, hangar and small terminal building. This small marine airport remained in service for many years until a land aerodrome was built on the island.

In pioneering South Atlantic services, between West Africa and South America, Lufthansa, the German airline, used Dornier Wal twin-engined flying-boats for the carriage of mail. These aircraft did not have the range to fly nonstop and therefore alighted close to depot ships. The ships, several of which were used, trailed aprons from their sterns on-to which the flying-boats were taxi-ed and then lifted aboard to be refuelled. They were then launched by large catapults because they could operate at higher weights when catapulted than they could when taking-off from the sea. The experiments began in May 1933, scheduled mail services began in February 1934 and the 100th scheduled Wal flight took place in August 1935.

The establishment of air services across the North Atlantic was extremely difficult. The distance involved was great and the frequent very strong winds considerably increased it on westbound flights. Ireland and Newfoundland were the obvious terminal points of the transocean sector but the distance between them was excessive for the aircraft of the period and various ways of overcoming the problem were given close attention. Surveys were made of routes via Iceland and Greenland and via the Azores and Bermuda. There was also much talk of anchoring seadromes in the ocean. These would have been large pier-like floating structures with large flat decks on which landplanes could have landed to refuel. For a variety of reasons it is extremely unlikely that this system could have worked.

The only practical solution was the production of aircraft with sufficient range for nonstop flight while having the ability to carry at least some payload, and it was with these – the Short C class and Sikorsky S-42 flying-boats – that Imperial Airways and Pan American conquered the North Atlantic. Southampton was the United Kingdom terminal, there were simple facilities at Botwood in Newfoundland and on the Shannon River in southern Ireland and, by the time passenger services started, there was a marine terminal at LaGuardia Airport, New York.

In 1934 the United Kingdom Government

◀ Pan American Airways' second marine airport at Dinner Key, Miami, Florida, in 1932. Two Sikorsky S-40 flying-boats are alongside the embarkation jetties.

decided that as far as was practicable all first class mail to British territories should be carried by air without surcharge. To carry the much bigger loads it was necessary for Imperial Airways to acquire a fleet of what were then high capacity aircraft. The use of landplanes would have involved construction of a large number of all-weather airports capable of handling heavy aircraft, and to avoid this expense it was decided to operate the trunk routes to South Africa, India, Malaya and Australia with flying-boats and a fleet of Short C class four-engined monoplanes was ordered, the first being commissioned in the autumn of 1936.

These flying-boats worked from Southampton Water across France to the combined land-and-marine airport at Marignane near Marseilles, then across the Mediterranean via Lake Bracciano in the hills near Rome, to Athens and Alexandria where the African and eastern routes diverged. From Alexandria the flying-boats continued up the Nile and then via Lake Victoria to the coast at Mombasa where they turned south to terminate at Durban.

On the eastern route the C class flying-boats crossed the desert to Lake Habbaniyeh, west of Baghdad, and called at the Margil combined land-and-marine airport at Basra before flying down the Gulf and along the Baluchistan coast to Karachi.

The Margil combined land-and-marine airport at Basra, Iraq, with the Short C class flying-boat *Coriolanus* at moorings.

Lakes at Raj Samand and Gwalior served as alighting areas on the flight across India to the Ganges at Allahabad. The Hooghli River served the flying-boats at Calcutta, after which they flew via Burma, Thailand and Malaya to the combined land-and-marine airport at Singapore. Here Qantas Empire Airways' C class flying-boats took over for the flight through the Netherlands East Indies to Darwin, and then via the Gulf of Carpentaria to Townsville, Gladstone, Brisbane and Sydney.

At most places on these flying-boat routes the aircraft were moored to buoys and passengers were taken ashore by launches to hotels or to resthouses – some of which were houseboats. Launches provided radio control and patrolled alighting areas to ensure that they were free from driftwood and other obstructions which could tear the bottoms out of the flying-boats. There were also refuelling launches. Flarepaths were laid out in parallel rows when night operations were required.

On the Shatt al Arab at Basra the flying-boats were moored close to the terminal building which also served the land airport, and at Singapore there was a hangar for flying-boats and slipways at the new airport which was opened in 1937. There was also a hangar and slipway at Kisumu on Lake Victoria. At Rose Bay, Sydney, Qantas built a passenger terminal with embarkation jetties, a large hangar and a slipway. This terminal still exists. The Southampton terminal is described later in this chapter.

In April 1940 the long-planned air link between New Zealand and Australia was inaugurated by Tasman Empire Airways' C class flying-boat *Aotearoa*, and this flying-boat and the *Awarua*, operating between the Auckland terminal and Rose Bay, maintained throughout the war the *only* passenger service of any kind between the two countries.

For several years after the war BOAC, successor to Imperial Airways, continued to operate flying-boats, but with the South African service terminating at a base at Vaaldam to serve Johannesburg. For some time, too, Aquila Airways operated flying-boat services between Southampton and Madeira and to Capri and other Italian destinations, but the only real flying-boat bases used were those at Southampton and Marseilles. In the Australasian and South Pacific areas seaplanes and flying-boats continued to operate for many years to places which were without landplane facilities.

Even in 1972 a flying-boat was still used to maintain services between Sydney and Lord Howe Island where the lagoon was used as the alighting area. A hut and a jetty served as the terminal and the flying-boat was moored to a buoy. For many years after the war seaplanes were used to serve some of the communities in Papua, and it was during a

The BOAC Short Sandringham *Saint Andrew* and the passenger jetties at Vaaldam marine airport which served Johannesburg until the withdrawal of flying-boat services at the end of 1950.

flight on one of these routes, in 1959, that the author discovered what was almost certainly one of the most primitive 'marine airports' – it was at Esa 'Ala and consisted of a number of wooden planks filling the gap between the two hulls of an old catamaran. The seaplanes tied up to this and passengers were brought by launch from the shore about a mile away.

Throughout much of the period of British flying-boat operations the main United Kingdom terminal was in the Southampton area. A small terminal

building and a slipway at Woolston on the River Itchen served the flying-boats which flew the Guernsey route from 1923, and when the C class flying-boats were introduced a base was built at Hythe on the west side of Southampton Water. There was a hangar and slipway and an embarkation jetty. The next stage was a floating jetty with two platforms moored out in Southampton Water. The flying-boats were manoeuvred into this for loading and passengers transferred to it by launch from Southampton. The last pre-war development was a great improvement, and consisted of a raft moored at right angles to the dockside at Berth 108 at Southampton docks with a sloping ramp leading to the dock. A passenger handling unit was provided in one of the shipping sheds and trains took the passengers to and from London.

During the war flying-boats worked from Poole in Dorset and afterwards from Hythe, but in April 1948 a new terminal was provided at Berth 50 in Southampton docks. This comprised a passenger terminal and two U-shaped flying-boat docks into which the aircraft were winched stern first. BOAC operated its Solents there until November 1950 and Aquila Airways used the terminal until the end of British flying-boat operations on 30 September 1958.

Before the war there was a scheme for a large marine airport at Langstone Harbour, near Portsmouth. This was to have had three dredged take-off channels and two taxi-channels but no preparation work was ever done. The project was revived after the war and there were similar projects for a Thames site near Gravesend and another at the confluence of the Solent and Southampton Water. But no large-scale marine airport was ever built in Britain and neither were any of the proposed automatic flying-boat docking systems ever used.

Using facilities no different to those of the early days, flying-boats and seaplanes are still used in small numbers in various parts of the world, and recently experiments have been conducted using flying-boats to provide commuter services between Long Island Sound communities and Manhattan. These could lead to a partial revival of commercial flying-boat operations, but facilities would almost certainly be simple.

The Southampton marine airport terminal at Berth 50, with a
Short Solent flying-boat at the lefthand jetty.

15

Heliports

Heliport is the usual term for a specially prepared area from which helicopters operate – it is also known as a helistop and a helipad. In theory the helicopter, with its ability to take-off and land vertically as well as hover without forward speed, can operate from any space only slightly larger than itself and, in fact, military helicopters have landed in spaces smaller than themselves by first using their rotors to lop off branches from trees. But for safe operation, especially in built-up areas, the helicopter must be provided with an adequate and unobstructed landing area and preferably one with a wind direction indicator, firefighting equipment, and some form of lighting for night flying.

The site for a heliport, its size and the extent of its equipment is dependent on a number of factors. These are governed by the use to which it is to be put, the availability of land, the nature of the surrounding area – particularly in towns and cities – and the cost of construction that can be justified.

The variety of helicopter landing places is considerable. At airports it is usual to designate a landing area for helicopters and simply paint the approved form of marking on the ground. In country areas it is frequently sufficient to fence in a grass area and provide it with identification markings and a wind direction indicator. In some places landing pads have been erected above rivers, in others they are on elevated structures, and a few heliports have been built on roof-tops. In the case of helicopters working for the oil and gas industries they operate from small landing platforms on the offshore drilling rigs.

A precise figure for the number of heliports is not known, although it is known that in 1968 there were

◀ The Wall Street Heliport over the East River in New York City. Two helicopters can be seen on the taxiway.

1,812 in the United States, plus some 5,000 used by the Forest Service and that the number was increasing by several hundred a year. Out of the 1,812 heliports in the USA in 1968, all but 158 were at ground level and only 48 were situated on roof-tops. It is obviously cheaper to provide heliports at ground level; if they do have to be elevated structures it has been found that costs of construction and servicing rise steeply if the height of the heliport exceeds 100 ft (30 m).

With very few exceptions all the scheduled passenger and mail services operated by the helicopter airlines have been worked from ground level sites, although post office roofs have been used for mail services in Chicago and Los Angeles and for experimental flights in Moscow. In New York services were worked from the roof of the Pan Am Building to an elevated heliport at the 1965–66 World's Fair.

There are no internationally agreed standards for heliports, but the International Civil Aviation Organization (ICAO) has produced a manual to give guidance on all aspects of heliports and the United States, the United Kingdom, Japan and some other countries have published their own recommended practices.

The take-off and landing area of public heliports, according to United States recommendations, should have a length at least equal to twice the overall length of the largest helicopter using the heliport, and the area's width should be equal to at least one and a half times the length of the helicopter. The landing area should be suitably marked. In the case of circular heliports the diameter should be equal to the larger dimension. The actual touchdown area should be of a size equal to the rotor diameter of the helicopter, but for small helicopters an area measuring 6m (20 ft) by 6m has been found sufficient. The actual touchdown surface must of course be able to bear the maximum impact loading which could be put upon it by a helicopter under emergency conditions.

The landing area should be marked to outline its extent and a large cross composed of four triangles, their points meeting in the centre, should appear in the centre. This replaces the formerly used letter H enclosed in a triangle which is now regarded as acceptable only for private-use heliports. A wind direction indicator should always be provided and this should be illuminated for night operation. Also for night flying, the perimeter of the heliport should be lit, as should any obstructions, and there should be an identification beacon.

If a heliport is used in bad weather when instrument approaches are necessary it must have a system of lights to guide the pilot. These consist of lines of

Westland Heliport London with the landing pad seen above the mud of the Thames at low tide.
The boundary and obstruction lights can be seen, with the small terminal building
beyond the taxiway ramp.

lights to mark the landing area, a line of approach
lights set across the heliport, perimeter floodlights
and two-colour visual approach slope indicators to
guide the helicopter's angle of descent.

A major problem in siting a heliport is ensuring
that there are unobstructed flight paths leading to
and from the landing area so that helicopters may
make safe approaches and departures without risk

to their occupants or to those on the ground. These paths should also enable the helicopters to operate without creating a disturbance by noise or the downwash from their rotors. It should also be ensured that the heliports are not subject to turbulence caused by high buildings.

These are some of the ideals for heliports, but many of the early heliports were built before the formulation of these practices and most of them have been operated successfully and with good safety records.

The pioneers of regular scheduled helicopter services were the United States, the United Kingdom and Belgium. Los Angeles Airways, in 1947, was the first to run such services, initially for mail carriage, when that airline flew Sikorsky S-51s within a 50-mile (80 km) radius of the main Los Angeles post office from whose roof it operated. Two years later Helicopter Airways (later Chicago Helicopter Airways) began a similar service in the Chicago area with Bell 47s. In 1952 New York Airways, using the larger Sikorsky S-55, began mail services and in the following year began carrying passengers. By the end of 1956 all three companies were flying passenger services linking their city's various airports, and these airports with the cities themselves and some of their suburbs.

At the airport the helicopters operated from

designated sections of the terminal areas but elsewhere they used small fenced-in sites which had a paved landing area and a wind direction indicator.

In New York the Port Authority built the West 30th Street Heliport beside the Hudson River. This comprised two small landing pads over the water, a taxiway connecting the two, and a modest passenger terminal and office. This heliport was large enough to handle the twin-rotor Vertol 44 when it was introduced into service. After some years the helicopter services were transferred to the downtown business area near Wall Street where one of the piers over the East River was converted into a heliport with landing pad, taxiway and terminal. Then came a much more ambitious scheme – a heliport 800 ft (245 m) up, on the roof of the Pan Am Building in central Manhattan, with a landing area of 121 ft (37 m) by 113 ft (34 m). Services began from there in 1965 but after a while these operations to Manhattan were suspended and when they were resumed, in 1971, the heliport used was the one near Wall Street. The Pan Am Building heliport had a number of disadvantages, one of which was the turbulence caused by the neighbouring high buildings although metal vanes surrounding the landing area did smooth out much of the airflow over the actual landing pad.

In the United Kingdom it was British European Airways which pioneered helicopter services, from

January 1947. Dummy mail trials were undertaken in the west of England and followed by actual mail services in East Anglia, then in June 1950 BEA began the world's first regular passenger service with helicopters – from Liverpool to Cardiff with an intermediate landing at Wrexham. The airports were used as the Liverpool and Cardiff terminals, and Peterborough aerodrome served as headquarters of the East Anglia mail services; elsewhere landings were made on farms or in fields. In June 1951 the first British heliport came into operation when BEA began a London–Birmingham helicopter service. This heliport, known as Haymills Rotorstation, was on the outskirts of Birmingham and comprised a small fenced-in area with two small circular landing pads and a wooden passenger building.

Later, BEA was to use a number of heliports in various parts of Britain, including a circular grass area on the south bank of the Thames near Waterloo from which a short-lived helicopter service was operated to and from London Airport Heathrow.

The only heliport in Britain now used for regular passenger services is that at Penzance from where Sikorsky S-61Ns operate to and from the Scilly Islands. This heliport has a fairly large terminal building and a 100 ft (30 m) by 100 ft landing pad in the centre of a strip measuring about 900 ft (275 m) by 150 ft (45 m).

The original Brussels Allée Verte Heliport in 1953 before it was enlarged. The helicopter on the taxiway is a Sabena Sikorsky S-55.

London has a heliport but it is not used by any scheduled services. This is known as Westland Heliport London and is situated on the south bank of the Thames near Battersea. The landing pad, built over the river, measures 125 ft (38 m) by 53 ft (16 m) and can take helicopters of up to 36,000 lb (16,330 kg) weight. A taxiway leads to a parking area large enough for several small helicopters. There are night flying facilities, air traffic control and a terminal building – there is also a rescue launch!

In Belgium, Sabena began a network of helicopter mail services in 1950 and in 1953 started passenger services linking Brussels, Antwerp, Rotterdam, Lille, Liége and Maastricht. Later Paris, Cologne and Bonn were served as well. For the mail services a series of very simple heliports was prepared; in Brussels for example, this was a 45 m (150 ft) square fenced-in grass area with a small asphalt landing pad, a post office hut and a simple wind indicator. But when passenger services began, with S-55s, much larger heliports were used. In Brussels the heliport was in the centre of the city and beside the Allée Verte railway terminus. There was a terminal building with customs and immigration facilities and close to it a parking area for several helicopters. From this a taxiway led to the 20 m (65 ft) square landing pad. This site was large enough for the helicopters to take-off and fly backwards for some distance before beginning their forward climb, thus ensuring that they attained safety speed within the confines of the heliport. Later still the Allée Verte heliport itself was enlarged. It had a new terminal 31 m (just over 100 ft) long, in front of which was a parking apron measuring 121 by 38 m (397 by 125 ft) and this was connected by three short taxiways to a long 7 m (23 ft) wide taxiway which connected three 25 m (82 ft) diameter landing pads. The total length of the heliport was 588 m (1,930 ft) and it has

been known to handle at least six Sikorsky S-58s at one time. Most of the other heliports used by Sabena were of much simpler design, but the one in Rotterdam also had taxiways linking three circular landing pads although they were only 12·5 m (41 ft) in diameter.

There have in fact been very few sustained helicopter airline operations. Those mentioned in the United States have been joined by services in the San Francisco Bay area; there have been a number of routes operated in Italy; there are some in Greenland, and there have been services between Melbourne Airport and a city heliport over the Yarra.

The Soviet Union makes very large-scale use of helicopters and has many regular passenger services, but virtually nothing is known about Soviet heliports except that there is one in Moscow beside the airline town terminal.

In 1963 Pakistan International Airlines began to develop a helicopter network in what was then East Pakistan. This was based on Dacca and served numerous points including a route stretching 170 miles (273 km) from Dacca through Barisal, Hatia and Sandwip to Chittagong. At Dacca the Sikorsky S-61Ns operated from one of the airport taxiways, but elsewhere fenced-in heliports were constructed and these had landing pads, wind stockings, firefighting equipment and passenger buildings. Unfor-

The floating heliport on the Yarra River at Melbourne. A Trans-Australia Airlines Bell 47J is seen landing.

tunately, two helicopters were lost in accidents, one on a training flight, and the service was closed down.

All heliports used for regular services, with the exception of Brussels, have been quite small, many only designed for the operation of one helicopter at any particular time, but as larger helicopters enter service and higher frequency services are developed we can expect heliports of greater sophistication.

The really economic commercial helicopter, suitable for scheduled services in high density traffic areas, has been promised for a long time but has yet to make its appearance. The helicopter manufacturers cannot afford to develop such a vehicle – which should possibly have about 100 seats – without the promise of good airline orders and the airlines do not have the money to spend.

But if and when such vehicles do come into operation, they will require quite large heliports capable of handling several machines simultaneously. This means that there must be adequate aircraft parking areas well clear of the actual landing pads, and it is increasingly difficult to find such sites in cities. It will be necessary to provide some form of instrument landing system and perhaps a more sophisticated lighting system, and, to give clear flight paths to and from the heliport, where possible it is likely that the bigger ones will be sited close to or over rivers and other waterways.

16

STOLports and Altiports

Most of the aircraft employed in the early days of air transport would have come within today's definition of STOL – Short Take-Off and Landing – but as aircraft became heavier their demands on aerodrome and runway lengths became ever greater. For many years STOL aircraft have been used for specialised rôles but now STOL is seen as a partial solution to overcoming ground and air congestion by the provision of short runways capable of handling STOL aircraft which can bring air services close to the cities.

A string of STOLports has been built along the Norwegian coast and these are used by Widerøe's de Havilland Canada Twin Otters to provide air transport to communities where longer runways are prohibited by terrain.

Separate STOL runways are beginning to appear at major airports, so that STOL aircraft can operate without using the runways, taxiways and flight paths of the conventional aircraft. One of the first of these special STOL runways was that at New York's LaGuardia Airport.

STOLports have already been established in many areas, there are some in the United States, in the Caribbean, New Guinea, Nepal, and there is one on the German island of Heligoland. Most of these are simply short runways of varying quality, although some like that at Clear Lake in Texas are really miniature airports with terminal, hangar, car parking and other facilities.

There is disagreement about the recommended length for a STOL runway but an accepted figure is about 2,000 ft (609 m) for a paved runway at sea level in temperatures of up to 90 degrees F (32·2

◀ An Air-Alpes Pilatus Turbo-Porter on the altiport at Val d'Isère. The tracks of the aircraft can be seen where it turned after finishing its uphill landing run.

degrees C). The length should be increased for unpaved runways, runways at higher elevations or where higher temperatures are encountered.

It is likely that during the next few years STOL transport systems may come into being in a number of areas and that STOLports will be built, some at ground level and some as elevated structures, with full instrument and lighting facilities for all-weather operation. A number of transport aircraft have been designed to operate from this type of facility.

An unusual development of the STOLport is the Altiport. This is really a STOLport high in the mountains. For some years the French airline Air-Alpes has been operating regular services to a number of altiports in the French Alps. The Air-Alpes services, flown by Swiss Pilatus Turbo-Porters, Twin Otters, and some smaller aircraft, operate from standard airports at lower levels carrying winter sports passengers to the altiports. When necessary, combination wheel/ski undercarriages are used.

A typical altiport is that at Courcheval which is at an elevation of 2,016 m (6,614 ft). The runway has a length of 260 m (850 ft) with an average slope of 20 per cent and a maximum slope of as much as 30 per cent, and its lower threshold is right on the edge of a steep drop into a valley. As in New Guinea, all landings must be made uphill and take-offs downhill regardless of the wind direction.

The special STOL runway at LaGuardia Airport, New York.

17

D/FW 2001, and the Future

The airport of the future can perhaps best be portrayed by a description of the projected D/FW 2001, the title used for the ultimate stage of the Dallas/Fort Worth Regional Airport in Texas, for although the airport is due to open in the second half of 1973, with completion of the first phase of construction scheduled for 1975, the overall plan is so extensive and the project on such a vast scale that it is the first to provide a true glimpse of the airport of the twenty-first century.

First it is necessary to establish just how enormous this new airport will be when completed. It will measure 9 miles (14·5 km) from north to south and 8 miles (12·8 km) from east to west, and the line of passenger terminals will be 4 miles (6·4 km) in length. If this airport were turned through 90 degrees and built in London, it would stretch from Hammer-smith in the west to Greenwich in the east; if built on Manhattan it would occupy the area from the Bronx to Battery Park and it would be nearly four times the width of the entire Manhattan Island.

The Dallas/Fort Worth Airport has been planned on the assumption that it could have to handle twenty million passengers and a million tons of cargo a year by 1985 with figures of about 40 million passengers and perhaps $3\frac{1}{2}$ million tons of cargo by the end of the century. Initially there will be four terminals for the handling of passengers and cargo, and three runways together with associated taxiways and apron areas. The initial terminals will be in the centre of what will eventually become a central spine comprising thirteen passenger terminals. On each side of this terminal area there will be a north–south main runway measuring 11,400 ft (3,475 m)

in length. On the eastern side of the airport there will be a crosswind runway aligned 13–31 (southeast–northwest) and this will initially be 9,000 ft (2,743 m) long.

In its final form the boundaries of the airport will enclose more than 17,000 acres (6,800 hectares) and the runways, taxiways and terminals will occupy about 8,500 acres (3,400 hectares).

When the airport is complete the main operational area will comprise a rectangle measuring about 4 miles (6·4 km) north to south by 2 miles (3·2 km) east to west, having diagonal extensions on each side to contain the crosswind runways and maintenance areas. The main rectangle will enclose the four main runways, taxiways and terminals, and extensions at each end will comprise cargo terminals, more maintenance areas, remote car parking, the post office complex and other facilities.

The runways have been planned to handle 153 aircraft movements an hour in visual flight rule (VFR) conditions in 1975, with up to 117 movements under instrument conditions (IFR). The ultimate aim is 266 movements in a peak hour, with 178 under IFR conditions. To handle this traffic there will be two sets of north–south parallel runways and two southeast–northwest crosswind runways. There will be a pair of north–south runways each side of the central terminal spine and the crosswind run-

ways will be one on each side of the airport. The outer north–south runways (18R–36L and 18L–36R) will initially be 13,400 ft (4,084 m) long with provision for extension to 20,000 ft (6,096 m) and the original north–south runways (17R–35L and 17L–35R) can be extended to 13,400 ft (4,084 m). It will be noted that the sets of main runways are not precisely parallel – there being 10 degrees difference in their alignment. The crosswind runways (13L–31R and 13R–31L) will be 9,000 ft (2,743 m) long, with provision to extend them to 11,000 ft (3,352 m). There will be 1,000 ft (305 m) paved overrun areas at the end of each runway. Clear zones will be reserved to allow installation of instrument landing systems at both ends of all six runways if required. A very extensive system of taxiways, with high-speed turnoffs, will be constructed and three sets of taxiways through the terminal area will link the two halves of the airport. It is envisaged that with winds from the north or south, take-offs will be made from the inner north–south runways and from one crosswind runway, with the take-off being made away from the terminal area. Landings will be on the outer north–south runways and on the crosswind runway towards the terminals. In strong crosswinds the southeast–northwest runways would be used with take-offs away from and landings towards the terminals.

◀ The Dallas/Fort Worth Regional Airport under construction in 1972.

In addition to the main runway pattern, the plan calls for a 5,000 ft (1,524 m) north–south (16L–34R) runway for executive and general aviation aircraft and two 2,500 ft (762 m) runways (16R–34L and 13R–31L) for STOL aircraft. These runway systems would have their own terminals, with the departure lounges for STOL services possibly underground with escalators to the loading area.

The passenger terminals are to be approximately semi-circular and twelve of them will be in pairs divided by the spinal road and the thirteenth opposite a transport service centre. By 1975 the terminals will provide 65 aircraft gate-positions and ultimately there will be 234 gates each capable of handling a Boeing 747 or similar aircraft. One terminal will be an international arrivals building and near it will be the 200-ft (60 m) high control tower.

A road system will serve the entire airport with separate arrival and departure levels at each terminal. An inter-city rapid transport system will run the length of the airport and connect it with Dallas, Fort Worth and other local communities, and some kind of internal transport system is planned to serve the entire airport including each terminal. This latter would carry passengers, cargo and mail, and would probably be linked with the urban transport system to create a fully automated airport.

In the ultimate plan there is provision for two vast

cargo terminals, one at each end of the airport, and each would have 100 loading-gates for aircraft of up to 300 ft (91 m) wing span. Maintenance areas will occupy a large area; there is to be a world trade centre, a spiritual centre and even an aviation museum. There will be parking space for 27,000 vehicles by 1980, by which time nearly 1,500 scheduled air services are expected to be operating every day.

Dallas/Fort Worth Airport, like Roissy-en-France and the new Tokyo airport are, in their initial stages, airports of the present or at least of the very near future; but the scale of their planning means that they are also very much airports of the more distant future, airports which will render major service in the early years of the next century.

However, aircraft development is extremely rapid and it is always difficult to foretell accurately the shape of air transport more than a few years hence. Until the end of the 1960s the biggest commercial aircraft weighed about 350,000 lb (158,760 kg) but then in 1970 came the Boeing 747 which already has a take-off weight of 775,000 lb (351,530 kg), and for some years the 1,000,000 lb (453,590 kg) aeroplane has been regarded as a certainty within the next decade. In mid-1972 Boeing was studying an enormous oil-carrying aircraft with twelve large engines, a wing span of 480 ft (146 m) and a payload of

Dallas/Fort Worth Regional Airport as it is planned for the ▶ beginning of the twenty-first century. The curved terminal buildings can be seen spaced along the central spine road, with the runway systems on each side.

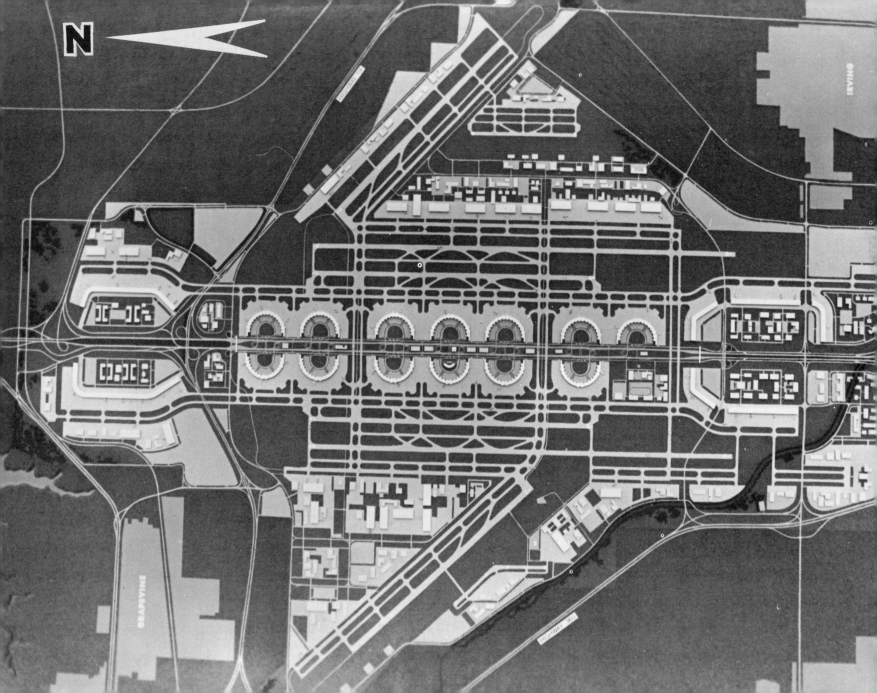

2,300,000 lb (1,043,300 kg). Such an aircraft would have a take-off weight almost certainly in excess of 5,000,000 lb (2,268,000 kg) and would require much wider, and probably stronger, runways than any so far built or planned.

Shortage of land in many areas would appear to make provision of much longer runways unlikely and we can expect a much greater effort to reduce take-off and landing runs, with a consequent increase in traffic at smaller airports. We may also see STOL or RTOL (Reduced Take-Off and Landing) aircraft landing on one end of a runway and taking-off from its other end.

However, the future growth of traffic, regardless of the types of aircraft used, ensures that runway, taxiway, apron and terminal capacity will constantly expand.

VTOL aircraft could drastically change the pattern of airports because they will not require runways, but it is impossible to forecast whether we shall ever achieve vertical take-offs and landings with high-capacity long-range transport aircraft, although this category of short-range aeroplane could be in service in some numbers within the next fifteen to twenty years. Although these aircraft would reduce the demand for runways they will still require all the other airport facilities on a considerable scale.

Whatever the future pattern, it is likely that we shall see an increase in the number of airports, with the bigger cities perhaps having several around their perimeters.

Perhaps the best forecast that we can make for the remainder of this century is that aircraft will become bigger but will for the most part require facilities comparable to those of the present, with towards the end of the century a gradual introduction of VTOL aircraft. STOL operations can be expected to increase during this time but only for short-stage operations. We can also expect to see at least one runway provided in the United States for landings by space shuttles and their launchers as they return from earth orbits. However, these vehicles are unlikely to require facilities much different to those now demanded by the big commercial jet aircraft.

INDEX OF PRINCIPAL AIRPORTS

SOME LEADING AIRPORTS

(with traffic figures for 1970)

Airport	Longest runway	Elevation	Aircraft movements	Passengers	Cargo (tons)
Chicago - O'Hare, USA	11,600 ft	667 ft	641,390	29,689,000	532,000
Los Angeles International, USA	12,090 ft	126 ft	544,025	20,781,000	400,000
Atlanta, USA	10,000 ft	1,024 ft	426,392	16,627,000	188,000
Dallas, USA	8,800 ft	485 ft	410,154	10,450,000	100,000
San Francisco International, USA	10,600 ft	11 ft	386,674	14,448,000	317,000
New York - John F. Kennedy, USA	14,572 ft	12 ft	365,848	19,097,000	760,000
Washington National, USA	6,870 ft	15 ft	319,449	9,400,000	39,000
New York - LaGuardia, USA	7,000 ft	21 ft	297,652	11,845,000	40,000
London - Heathrow, UK	12,800 ft	80 ft	270,302	15,607,000	369,806
Miami International, USA	10,500 ft	9 ft	253,813	10,661,000	256,912
Boston - Logan, USA	10,090 ft	19 ft	244,591*	9,389,000	146,000
Toronto International, Canada	11,050 ft	569 ft	220,996	6,000,000	80,000
New York/New Jersey - Newark, USA	8,200 ft	18 ft	204,595	6,460,000	157,000
Frankfurt - Rhein Main, Germany	12,795 ft	368 ft	195,802	9,402,000	360,874
Paris - Orly, France	11,975 ft	292 ft	191,014	10,382,000	194,362
Rome - Leonardo da Vinci, Italy	12,800 ft	7 ft	167,981	7,453,000	—
Tokyo International, Japan	10,335 ft	8 ft	163,612	10,362,000	200,000
Copenhagen - Kastrup, Denmark	10,827 ft	16 ft	156,757	6,466,000	124,442
Amsterdam - Schiphol, Netherlands	11,330 ft	—13 ft	135,520	5,172,000	189,986
Zürich, Switzerland	12,139 ft	1,414 ft	130,472	4,530,000	106,064
Geneva - Cointrin, Switzerland	12,795 ft	1,411 ft	113,076	2,779,000	29,550
Brussels National, Belgium	11,936 ft	180 ft	96,404	2,836,000	103,177
Hongkong - Kai Tak, HK	8,350 ft	15 ft	87,013	2,325,000	61,186

* Air transport movements only.   Figures for Rome are Leonardo da Vinci and Ciampino combined.